Beading with Brick Stitch

DIANE FITZGERALD

A **BEADWORK**
HOW-TO BOOK

INTERWEAVE PRESS

Editor, Judith Durant
Technical editor, Dorothy T. Ratigan
Copy editor, Dena Twinem
Illustration, Gayle Ford
Photography, except as noted, Joe Coca
Page design and production, Dean Howes
Cover design, Bren Frisch

Interweave Press, Inc.
201 E. Fourth St.
Loveland, CO 80537-5655
USA

Printed in the United States by Kendall Printing Company

Library of Congress Cataloging-in-Publication Data

Fitzgerald, Diane.
    Beading with brick stitch : a beadwork how-to book / Diane Fitzgerald.
        p. cm.
    Includes index.
    ISBN 1-883010-72-1
        1. Beadwork--Patterns. I. Title.

TT860 .F55 2001
745.58'2—dc21   00-143854

First printing: IWP-10M:101:KPC

Contents

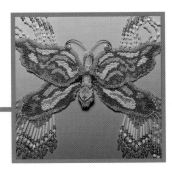

Acknowledgments

The kindness and generosity of many people helped bring this book about. My sincere appreciation goes to my special brick stitch class: Joanne Hite, Bonnie Voelker, Cheryl Erickson, Peggy Wright, Carol Perkins, Liana Magee, Susan Manchester, Doris Coghill, NancyLee Dahlin, Jane Langenback and Alois Powers; and also to my British friends Carole Morris, Stephney Hornblow, Vera Gray, Ann Mockford, Margret Carey and Stefany Tomalin; to my friends in South Africa, Stephen Long and Dr. Frank Jolles; to Judith Durant, my editor, who rigorously reviewed the text and made me look good with her thoroughness; to technical editor, Dot Ratigan, who reviewed the projects; and to publisher Linda Ligon for providing the wherewithal to bring the project to fruition; and finally to Virginia Blakelock, author of *Those Bad, Bad Beads* and Horace Goodhue (may he rest in bead heaven), author of *Indian Bead-Weaving Patterns*, both of whom personally and through their books, taught me the basics.

Introduction

I felt like I was on a roller coaster when Judith Durant of Interweave Press contacted me. Would I be interested in doing a book in a series on beadwork for Interweave? Would I? Wow! I sure would! The topic would be brick stitch. Oooh! That took the wind out of my sails. I had hoped it would be peyote stitch. Fortunately, I recalled a lesson from creativity guru Edward DeBono, "Always look for the second right answer," and my rational self began speaking to me. "Diane, these kind of opportunities don't come knocking on your door every day. Get over it. It's a chance to go in a new direction and learn new things." These thoughts flashed through my mind in less time than it takes to read them. Hopefully, without missing a beat, I responded, "Great! I'd love to. Let's do it!"

And so here we have it. The result of a year of work with the help of many people. In writing my first book, *Beads and Threads: A New Technique for Fiber Jewelry*, with Helen Banes, I learned a valuable lesson from the publisher, Seymour Bress of Flower Valley Press: To give the book depth, richness, and appeal, include the work of many people in addition to your own. I knew this book would be better if I had some moral support, so I put out a call to my Minnesota students asking for eight good beaders to take a class in brick stitch and be my "beta" testers over a period of several months. Eleven signed on (see acknowledgments). And so we began. I developed the projects and wrote instructions. The class tried them out and gave me feedback. With instructions for the basic design, the students would vary it with the size and shape of beads, take off in new directions, and come back in two weeks to show off their triumphs.

Sometimes there was a bit of frustration, like the class where we tried out the Sweet Little Bow Pin. That simple little project was the toughest one to nail down. (You should see my first sample!) The class was honest and frank. I remember the night we were supposed to make a three-dimensional figure in brick stitch. They were all kind of glum. Finally someone said, "Do we really have to do this? Most of us don't like making beaded faces because they always come out so ugly." There was a chorus of agreement so we switched gears to our next project, and the beaded faces ended up on the cutting room floor, so to speak. In contrast, the evening I brought out the Petroglyph Necklace there were oohs and aahs of glee around the table. This project had high appeal. Someone even said, "This one should go on the cover!" Over the sessions, the students learned the value of this versatile stitch. It was an experience I'll never forget and I owe them all a deep debt of gratitude.

And then, surprisingly, help came from an unexpected quarter. Through my English friend, Carole Morris, I was introduced via the Internet to two wonderful women, Stephney Hornblow and Vera Gray. They agreed to test some of my patterns for accuracy and Vera offered valuable suggestions about naming conventions for stitches.

As I tell all my students, I love to hear about your accomplishments using my designs and am happy to try to answer your questions. So if you would like to write to me, please do so. My address is Beautiful Beads, 115 Hennepin Ave., Minneapolis, MN 55401.

And there you have it. Like any project, one can't do it alone. I hope you enjoy our efforts!

First row, left to right: Liana Magee, Diane Fitzgerald, and Doris Coghill; second row: Cheryl Erickson, Carol Perkins, Joanne Hite, Bonnie Voelker, NancyLee Dahlin, Susan Manchester, Peggy Wright, and Jane Langenback; not present: Alois Powers.

History of Brick Stitch

Many beaders may be familiar with brick stitch from the "triangle" and "duster" earrings popular in the 1960s and 1970s. These earrings were often made with triangle tops, bugle beads, and graceful, flowing fringe according to patterns learned from friends or books. They were quick and easy to make and flattering to wear. These brick stitch earrings are still popular today and many patterns are available.

As a means of weaving seed beads, and even larger beads, brick stitch offers some unique results and many people love it for these reasons. Many beaders say brick stitch patterns are easier to follow because the rows are level (unlike peyote stitch where each row is offset from the next). This characteristic enables beaders to make concentric curving bands of color like the layers of an agate or geode. Many find it is easier to increase with

Triangle Earrings. In the 1960s and 1970s, triangle earrings or brick stitch earrings with long fringe seemed to be a de rigueur *part of hippies' or flower children's clothing. Patricia Bell models these for us. (Photo by the author.)*

brick stitch than other techniques when working around a shaped object. I love it because of the wonderful fabric that can be made with it using cylinder beads.

BRICK STITCH BEADWORK AROUND THE WORLD

We can never know who added the first bead to her work with the now familiar brick stitch, but we can surmise how it might have happened. Brick stitch, also sometimes known in the Americas as Comanche or Cheyenne stitch, is less like weaving and more like knitting or crochet in that the thread is connected to the row below and pulled up through a bead or beads to form the linkage. Basket makers could have inspired brick stitch as it somewhat resembles coiled basketry. Or maybe it was stitchers who did the blanket stitch to decorate the edge of a coverlet or the buttonhole stitch to secure the hole for a button. Someone else suggested that brick stitch

"IT IS NOT EASY TO READ history from things. They are illegible to those who know how to read only writing. They are mute to those who listen only for pronouncements from the past. But they do speak; they can be read." Steven Lubar and W. David Kingery, eds. *History From Things: Essays on Material Culture.* Washington D.C.: Smithsonian Institution Press, 1993.

may be related to the beaded wire baskets made in the seventeenth century. Connecting a bead to the edge could have been done with a technique similar to brick stitch even if other techniques were used for the rest of the basket. Whoever did it, we have them to thank for a wonderfully versatile stitch.

Until about twenty-five years ago, little was written about brick stitch. In older books, if it is mentioned at all, it may be referred to as an unusual type of peyote stitch. Brick stitch has generally played second fiddle to peyote stitch and netting. Unlike these stitches, which seem to be used everywhere there are seed beads, brick stitch has appeared only in small areas scattered around the world. Why this is so is anybody's guess. What made the tribes of the Eastern Cape of South Africa practice this beadwork technique, which is identical to that of the Southern Plains Indians of North America? Why was this stitch used so infrequently in most other places beadwork was done?

Let's take a look at how brick stitch has been used over time in different parts of the world.

Africa

Africa is well-known for its beaded adornments and beadwork; little wonder considering the supply of beads brought to this continent in the last several centuries. According to a publication of the South African National Gallery, *Ezakwantu: Beadwork From the Eastern Cape* (Capetown: 1993), between 1932 and 1955 alone, the Societa Veneziana Conterie of

Venice, Italy, shipped 3.7 million kilos of beads to Africa. Of these, almost half, or roughly 1.6 million kilos, were shipped to South Africa and Zimbabwe (then Rhodesia). It is likely that this amount would be at least doubled if we were to include the beads imported from Bohemia! Even before European beads were exported to Africa, beads had been traded into southern Africa for centuries, probably first by Phoenicians bringing Egyptian beads, and then later by Arabs bringing beads from India, and still later by the Portuguese bringing European beads. It is here, in Africa, that we can see some of the best beadwork done with brick stitch.

The Zulu

To the Zulu women of South Africa goes the prize for not only the most prolific use of brick stitch, but also for the most creative use. As a precious commodity, mysterious in production, glass beads were often reserved for royalty, thus making beads and beadwork items deserving of awe and respect.

Over time, beadwork became an intimate part of the Zulu culture. Most beadwork is made by young women who define the meanings of colors and patterns, but both men and women wear it. Young girls learn the language of beadwork as they visit a local store to buy beads. They learn about color and social sig-

Early on, Zulu children learn the significance of beadwork and wear it proudly. (Photo from the collection of Carole Morris, undated but probably about 1900.)

nificance by discussing the beadwork worn by others. Men learn the meaning of beadwork colors and patterns from female family members. The beadwork then communicates who has reached the various stages of courtship and marriage, as well as where a person lives. Beadwork thus becomes a sign proclaiming, "I am available," or "I am committed."

Although Zulu women use many off-loom beading techniques, most of their techniques are based on brick stitch or netting. However, they use these basic techniques with such unusual creative variations that, in

IDENTIFYING BRICK STITCH

I do not claim to be an authority on either brick stitch or beadwork, and in searching for material for this section of the book, it soon became apparent how difficult it is to determine whether a piece was made with brick stitch or peyote stitch. They look the same if you rotate one or the other a quarter turn. If you take a magnifying glass and look closely between the beads of any piece done with these stitches, you'll see what I mean. Many pieces done with brick stitch will look like peyote stitch because the thread bridge from the previous row is often pulled up inside the new bead, especially if the beader worked with tight tension. The result is that you see two threads entering and exiting each bead, just like peyote stitch, and the loop is hidden. Sometimes one has only a picture to look at and can only guess which stitch was used by analyzing which way the work would have been done most conveniently. Sometimes it's easy: A piece will have a broken bead and then it is clear which stitch was used. You will see either two threads lying parallel with peyote stitch or one thread looped around the other with brick stitch. (See the Tile Bead Mat on page 21.)

Even if you have the good fortune to see a museum collection firsthand, unless you pull the beads apart (which most curators aren't likely to allow!) or see where a bead was broken out, it is difficult to be sure of the stitch used. In the case of beadwork that has been buried for hundreds of years, such as ancient Egyptian beadwork, the thread may have disintegrated and only the position of the beads can give you a clue. If the straight edge is on the width of the piece and the uneven edge on the length, it may be brick stitch. If it is the opposite, the straight edge on the length and the uneven edge on the width, it may be peyote stitch. But even these are not hard and fast rules. So you just have to ask yourself, "Is it likely that this piece was done with brick stitch? Did the people who made it often use brick stitch? Could it be worked with another technique and get this result?"

Brick stitch worked from bottom to top.

Peyote stitch worked from bottom to top.

Peyote stitch rotated 90 degrees appears identical to brick stitch

my estimation, their beadwork is unsurpassed for structural intricacy. In addition to the simple rectangular pendants worn around the neck, Zulu women use diamond and triangle elements, short or long flowing fringe, swags and loops of beads, picot edgings, delightful baubles, and other shapes to vary their beadwork. And, of course, these beadwork techniques and patterns were transferred from woman to woman without written instruction, without videos, without color-coded diagrams, and without the Internet! In addition, they usually used sinew (which they made themselves) without a needle.

Many beaders may be familiar with the Zulu "love letter" pendants, usually made with brick stitch and attached to a safety pin. Colors were chosen to communicate or symbolize a message for a loved one to wear and remember. While many interpretations have been offered for the color meaning, it is just as likely that the color choice of the maker was unique to her situation. What is more interesting is that these simple rectangular pendants have been worn by Zulus for more than one hundred years. The postcard pictured on page 9 shows little boys wearing several pendants around their necks. A similar pendant is showcased in the South African National Gallery in Capetown. It had been the

Among Zulus, brick stitch is one of the most popular beading techniques. Their many variations of it are used in bracelets, armbands, necklaces, earrings, bandoliers, and aprons. (Collection of Dr. Frank Jolles. Photograph by Z. J. S. Ndimande & Son, January, 1974 Greytown, Natal.)

prize of an English soldier taken during the fierce colonial battles in South Africa and was recently returned from England. In faded graceful script, it still bears a tag which reads, "Brought from Natal, 1879."

Lionel PHM Marshall, South Africa's minister of arts, culture, science and technology, added this message, which is displayed with the piece:

I was deeply moved to see and handle the Zulu necklace worn by Zulu warriors. This

artifact, which was repatriated into the country, is a reminder of the creative talent of Zulu women. They expressed their deep feelings and support for their beloved ones through beadwork. The dominance of red beads symbolizes spiritual warmth and love. The necklace evoked heroic feelings to a person of Zulu stock. The necklace is a living symbol of a gallant Amabutho who fell at Ulundi on July 4, 1879.

It would be hard to find a group to whom beadwork has more meaning than the Zulus.

The Xhosa and Thembu

One of the important articles of clothing among the Xhosa and Thembu, who live on the Eastern Cape of South Africa, is a large rectangular piece of fabric worn as a shawl and colored a lovely deep golden yellow. Intricate bands of beads and buttons decorate the lower edge. When worn around the shoulders, it is held closed with a large brooch usually made of a giant safety pin (about 3.5 inches across) to which brick stitch beadwork, usually with a simple geometric pattern, has been attached. Below the beadwork, the most intriguing fringe is added made of strands with flowerets regularly interspersed. (Despite being shown how to do this, I still haven't succeeded in duplicating this marvelous technique!) A typical Xhosa woman might be seen with her head wrapped in a large turban and a long beaded pipe stuck in her mouth. (The extra length is said to be needed to keep ashes from falling on her breast or baby when she is nursing.) In the past, the pipe stem would have been covered in brick stitch, but today most pipe stems, if beaded, are simply wrapped with a strand of beads. Dangling from her wrist is a drawstring tobacco pouch, often heavily beaded as well.

Xhosa love to use white, pink, and both light and dark blue beads. They also make huge breastplate type pieces with solid beaded

Xhosa Decorative Shawl Pin. A safety pin, 3.5 inches long, is the base for this brick stitch and fringe piece. Note the flowerets on each strand of fringe. (Collection of the author.)

Xhosa Pendant Necklace. This is done in brick stitch with geometric designs, probably about 1920. (Collection of the author.)

fronts and swags of beads on the sides. According to Stan Schoeman in A *Brief History of Traditional African Bead Craft* (1996), among the Xhosa, special beadwork is used to denote different age sets, and distinctive beaded regalia is reserved for the bride and groom and their closely associated guests at their wedding.

The San

According to Margret Carey, a British authority on beadwork, the San (also known as Bushmen) are the oldest surviving group of people in southern Africa. They live much as they have for centuries in the Kalahari Desert—the women collecting seeds, fruit, vegetables, and larvae, while men hunt game with bows and arrows. (When I was in South Africa in 1998, I had planned a visit to the Kagga Kamma Nature Reserve where one could meet with Bushmen. Unfortunately, a contact there told me they had just taken a bus back to the Kalahari a few days earlier!) Today, one must travel to Namibia or Botswana to find San people who do brick stitch beadwork.

I learned through correspondence with Stephen Long, a collector and trader of African beadwork, that early San beadwork, and even some contemporary beadwork, consists of ostrich eggshell beads made into belts, headbands, and necklaces, sometimes strung, but more often made with brick stitch. Before they can have the fun of beadwork though, they have to make their own beads and thread. Ostrich eggs are broken into small pieces and pierced with a sharp awl. Several are strung on a piece of sinew and the rough edges chipped off. Next, the soft fiber from tree bark is twisted between the beads to make the string very taut and the rough edges are then further smoothed with a grooved stone (Pippa Skotnes, *Miscast: Negotiating the Presence of the Bushmen*). Sinew for thread is obtained from the animals killed for meat. Making sinew into thread involves removing the tendon from the back of an animal, drying it, separating it into strands of fiber, then

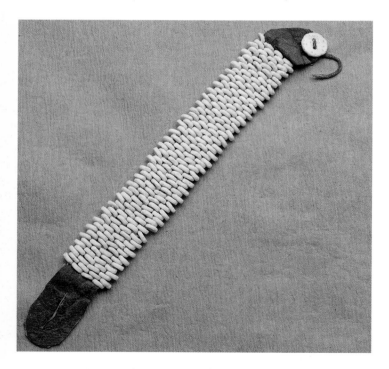

San (Bushman) Ostrich Eggshell Bracelet. Imagine not only making the beads, but the thread and leather for finishing as well! (Collection of the author.)

San (Bushman) Woman. The San transferred their brick stitch skills with ostrich eggshells to glass beads to make these colorful funnel-shaped and circular dangles for their hair. (From the Anthony Bannister Picture Library.)

MAKE YOUR OWN SAN (BUSHMAN) BAUBLES

Following the instructions for brick stitch given in the next chapter, begin with a row six beads wide. Work brick stitch for 14 rows, then increase at the end of each row for 14 more rows. Add a pattern in the center if you wish.

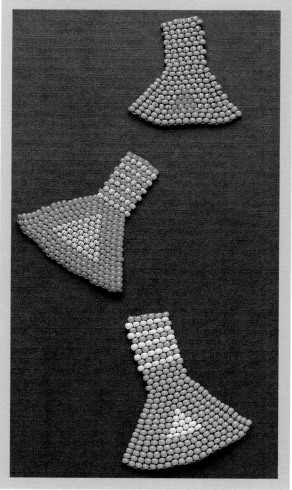

rolling two or more strands together to make a durable, sturdy thread. Because the sinew was fairly stiff, it could be used without a needle.

Recently, the San have used glass beads and brick stitch to make delightful funnel-shaped and circular pendants to wear in their hair and across their foreheads like a fringe. These same shapes, in opaque beads and bright primary colors, may be worn around the neck or attached to leather pouches as decoration. I tried making a funnel shaped bauble and somehow it made me feel connected to the San. Try it, you might have this feeling too!

I also learned from Mr. Long that other groups who specialize in brick stitch include the Ndebele (who are noted in the United States for the herringbone stitch), the Basotho, and the Shangaan/Tshangane. The latter two groups, while perhaps not as well known as the Zulus, make pieces that are unique to them. The Tshangane, one of the smallest tribes in South Africa, also use brick stitch to make pieces attached to very large safety pins, *xipereta*, which are worn on their skirts as decoration. Another brick stitch item that the Sotho use is a magnificent belt called *seqeleqele*, which is worn on top of an apron during an initiation ceremony.

The Kuba of West Africa

One Christmas, my husband gave me a delightful hat, which the seller attributed to the Kuba of Zaire, West Africa. It is pillbox-shaped and made with small Bohemian "tile" beads. (Shaped like small cylinders, these

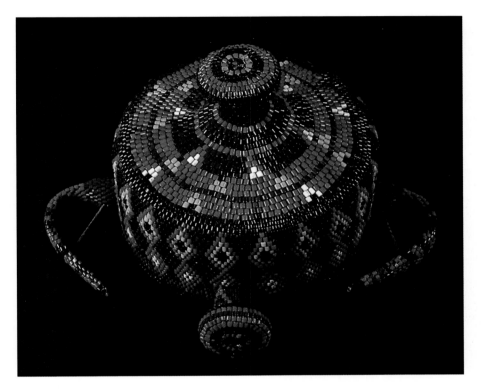

Kuba Hat. Knobs and horns give this hat distinctive and characteristic features. The Kuba live in Zaire, West Africa. (Collection of the author.)

beads were also known in Europe as Oriental beads.) Under the beadwork exterior, there is a basket-like form made of bark and twisted-fiber using a coiled basketry technique. The brick-stitch beadwork is worked on the surface of this "basket" in red, blue, yellow, and black diamond patterns. Beaded horns are added to each side and round knobs, also beaded, are added to the top, front, and back. (It's a little small for me, but I have worn it while dancing around the living room on occasion, much to the delight of my grandchildren.) A very similar hat is in the collection of the University of California Los Angeles Museum of Cultural Anthropology and is described as a chief's hat made by the Yaka of Zaire. (Arnoldi, Mary Jo and Christine Mullen Kreamer. *Crowning Achievements: African Arts of Dressing the Head* p. 22.) Margret Carey, in her book *Beads and Beadwork of West and Central Africa* (p. 47) notes that the Pende, also of Zaire, make similar hats .

Victorian Era Brick Stitch in Europe and America

The expression "Idle hands are the devil's workshop" typifies Victorian England. Sewing was a necessity for working-class women. In her book, *Victorian Embroidery*, Freda Parker tells us that both clothing and household goods were produced at home, with little spare money or time for bead embellishment. In contrast, she continues, elegant ladies did needlework and beadwork to please them, producing many items decorative and useful at that time such as bell pulls, fire screens, pen wipers, and blotters. Other items, such as beaded slippers, pillows, baskets, hair ornaments, purses, and clothing, may have been made for one's own use, or made to order from someone who did beading full time. While brick stitch was less popular than woven or embroidered beadwork, there is evi-

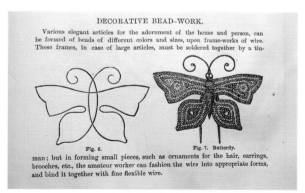

Beadwork Butterfly. Instructions for a beaded butterfly worked within a wire frame, probably with brick stitch. (1876 Ladies Fancywork, collection of the author.)

Victorian Tassels. Two tassels with long flowing fringe made with green iridescent three-cut beads and bugle beads (1" x 9"). Make your own with instructions on page 73. (Collection of the author.)

dence that it could have been one of the stitches used.

While instructions and designs were published in books and magazines of the day, they were often sketchy. Unlike today's instructions, which include text, diagrams, and even photos or videos, the Victorian beader was expected to be well-versed in handwork methods and be able to make an item simply by looking at a drawing of the finished piece.

I am fortunate to have parents that shared their interests and took mine just as seriously. My dad was an avid book collector and as he scanned the shelves of thrift stores or used-book stores he would watch for old books that might include beadwork for me. It was my dad who found the 1904 edition of Mary White's *How To Do Beadwork*, which covers many beadwork techniques, but not brick stitch, and also the 1876 *Ladies Fancywork: Hints and Helps to Home Taste and Recreations* by Mrs. C. S. Jones and Henry T. Williams. In the chapter "Decorative Beadwork" we find a diagram of a butterfly made with a wire frame. From looking at the position of the beads in the diagram, it seems likely that the beads were added to the wire with brick stitch using fine wire or horsehair and working from the outer edge toward the center. If you were making

a large butterfly, it was suggested that a tin-man could help you with the soldering!

As my dad searched for old books, my mother searched for old linens and needlework. When she went through the thrift stores, she would keep an eye out for examples of old

Victorian Purse. Bands of brick stitch are connected with a zigzag or lace stitch to make a simple but lovely purse. The drawstring is connected to the beadwork with metal rings. (Collection of Carole Morris, England.)

Victorian Velvet Tray. Tiny white seed beads look almost like snowflakes on the deep wine-colored velvet. Notice the variation of brick stitch along the edge. (Collection of the author.)

beadwork. Often at Christmas my present under the tree was a box of old beads and broken beadwork. In one of these boxes she included a pair of Victorian beaded tassels with a triangle top, just like the triangle earrings of the 1970s. They were probably used on a garment, or maybe hung below a bird cage or bell pull. I had forgotten about these tassels until I started writing this book and was delighted to see that they had a bit of brick stitch that could be used as an example. Instructions for a variation of these tassels are on page 73.

Another example of Victorian brick stitch is a purse loaned to me by my British friend and knowledgeable bead collector, Carole Morris. The purse is made of metal seed beads with cord drawstrings embellished with beaded tassels. These were connected to the purse with small metal rings. Vertical panels of brick stitch, which vary from one to three beads per row, are connected with a passementerie type of netting. The lower edge is finished with a looped fringe. Since the lining is nearly all missing, there is no label and it is not possible to know where it was made.

Several years ago, I happened on a delightful velvet tray, lovingly and delicately beaded primarily with white beads. The edge stitch is related to brick stitch, but has an extra bead between each stitch rounding it out and making the stitch more of a scallop. Many examples of Victorian-era beadwork that appear to be made with brick stitch can also be found in Waltraud Neuwirth's book,

Tile Bead Mat (detail). Broken beads may detract from the value of a piece like this, but the missing beads leave a telltale clue to the technique used to create the piece.

Tile Bead Mat. Used as a table decoration or protection. Making these mats was a popular pastime for adults and children in the 1920s and 1930s in both Europe and the United States. The colorful beads were relatively inexpensive and gave hours of pleasure to the beader creating a variety of patterns. (Collection of the author.)

Perlen Aus Gablonz. Written in German with an English translation, this book gives a detailed account of the Bohemian bead industry, and particularly the means of production. Neuwirth has also included many examples taken from *Harper's Bazaar* magazines of the late 1800s showing how beads were used in such items as lamp mats, rosettes, lamp collars, and purses. While we may think our contemporary beadwork is new, innovative, and unique, if we look at some of these Victorian examples, many of the structures, shapes, and techniques are similar to what we make and enjoy today.

A recent gift from my sister, Marilyn, was a real find, a large tile bead mat or trivet. In the last year or so, I had begun to collect these table decorations, which were made in the 1920s and 1930s and used to protect a table from a hot dish or a plant. This one, about twelve inches in diameter, is the largest I've ever seen. She almost passed it up at the antique store because several beads were broken and she was uncertain whether I could repair it. But the area where the beads were broken showed clearly that it had been done in brick stitch, a surprise to me. Most of the tile bead mats I had seen were made with peyote stitch according to instructions in kits sold widely by the Walco Company.

The beads used in these mats, known in the United States as tile beads, have an interesting history of their own. Although the process for making this type of pressed bead was probably invented by Richard Prosser in London about in 1840, the beads later took on the name of another man, a Mr. J. Felix Bapterosses, a Frenchman, who also made buttons as well as beads around 1870. The process involves compression of a finely ground mixture of clay, flint, and felspar into a mold. The material is then fired in a kiln. Cheap to produce, these popular beads flooded the European market and dealt a blow to the Bohemian bead business. But the Bohemian bead makers rallied quickly, and by 1885, the Redlhammer brothers had spent time with a chemistry teacher and worked out their own formula for making such beads. Until about 1960 when production was discontinued, the Czechs were the main producer of these beads.

Native American: The Comanche, Kiowa, and Southern Cheyenne

"During a peyote ceremony, which begins at sundown and continues through the night to close with a breakfast at dawn, the participants gather inside a tepee around a crescent-shaped altar. Important paraphernalia of the ceremony include the roadman's or leader's staff, which is said to represent a bow or lance, the fan, and the gourd rattle, as well as the fans the other participants hold in their hands."

The ceremony and items described above appear in a book by Georg J. Barth called *Native American Beadwork.* Most would have been beaded with brick stitch or peyote stitch. The Comanche, Kiowa, and southern Cheyenne who roamed the southern Great Plains in the eighteenth and nineteenth cen-

Native American Dance Fan. A fan is an important part of many Native American ceremonies and is often used by dancers at powwows or competitions. The graceful feathers and lavish beadwork give added dimension to any costume. (The Oklahoma Historical Society, State Museum of History. Photograph by Jeffrey Briley.)

turies practiced this ceremony and are noted for their use of brick stitch. In fact, the stitch is often referred to as Comanche stitch or Cheyenne stitch.

The buffalo was key to the survival of Native Americans, providing meat, robes, tepee covering, sinew thread, and water carriers made from the animal's stomach. Living outside the porcupine's habitat, the Great Plains dwellers did not have a quillwork tradition on which to base their beadwork when traders first began to bring European glass beads to this part of the country. Prior to using glass beads, there seems to be little evidence that these groups used brick stitch—they worked with shells, claws, seeds, bones, teeth, or stones as decoration. When they began doing beadwork, it was influenced more by painted hides, fringes, and attached metal cones, and later by the Woodland, Eastern, and Central Plains tribes who moved into Oklahoma's Indian Territory during the last half of the nineteenth century. So the brick stitch may have been introduced to them at the same time as glass beads. Brick stitch has been used more recently by Native Americans to cover secular items as well, such as key chains, pencils, pens, and

In his book *Beads and Beadwork of the American Indians,* William C. Orchard gives the following account of the coming of glass beads to America. Whether it is true or not is disputed, but it could have happened.

"The first record of the introduction of trade beads among the American Indians goes back to Columbus and his landing on Watling island on October 12, 1492. His log states:

Soon after a large crowd of natives congregated there.... In order to win the friendship and affection of that people, and because I was convinced that their conversion to our Holy Faith would be better promoted through love than through force, I presented some of them with red caps and some strings of glass beads, which they placed around their necks, and with other trifles of insignificant worth that delighted them and by which we have got a wonderful hold on their affections.

October 15. A man from Conception Island was presented with a red cap and a string of small green glass beads. (From a translation of Las Casas's abridgment of Columbus's First Voyage in Fox, G.V., An Attempt to Solve the Problem of the First Landing Place of Columbus in the New World, pp. 354-55, 360, Washington, 1882.)"

cigarette lighters (Lois Sherr Dubin in *North American Indian Jewelry and Adornment*).

William C. Orchard may be the first, or at least among the first, to provide written information with diagrams for brick stitch as used by Native Americans. His book, *Beads and Beadwork of the American Indians*, which first appeared in 1929, is considered a classic reference on Native American beadwork. He describes several items made with brick stitch:

1) a necklace with extremely small glass beads from Guatemala.
2) a small bag of woven beadwork made by a Comanche Indian for holding cornhusks cut to shape for use as cigarette wrappers, ornamented with a wave-like design and various colored beads.
3) two other specimens collected from the Ute, one a chipped stone knife-blade or spear point and the other a stone arrow point. The decorated parts were first covered with cotton cloth fitted tightly to the object.

Horace Goodhue, who is also well-known for his documentation of Native American use of various stitches in his book *Indian Bead-Weaving Patterns*, did not include brick stitch until his third edition. Goodhue spent a good part of his life collecting off-loom weaving techniques and was probably the first to give written form to many of them. Although not Native American himself, he developed a kindred spirit with them through the Boy Scouts. In the 1984 edition of his book, he describes brick stitch for the first time as follows: "...there is another peyote weave, which I have heard called the *Paiute* version. In it the beads are turned another way... Since it is easy to change the number of beads from row to row, it is useful in covering an irregular object. (I learned it from a doll bootee.)"

Goodhue's description shows that the first row is simply a strand of beads and that the second row is attached by looping around the thread between the beads of the first row, then back up through the last bead. In this way, the beads of the first row lie perpendicular to the beads of the second and subsequent rows. In his fourth edition, published in 1984, he adds instruction for a triangle base and includes a base row made of bugles with a two-needle ladder. In addition, Goodhue's instruction shows adding only one bead at the beginning of a row (rather than two), leaving the thread exposed. This gives the same appearance as edge decreasing in peyote stitch and could result in confusion when trying to identify a beadwork method from merely observing a finished piece and not looking between the rows of beads.

As I teach classes and do my own beadwork, I often wonder what it will be like for someone at the end of the twenty-first century as they go antique hunting and begin to find the wealth of beadwork we are producing as we begin the new millennium. I know how excited I am when I find a beaded "Whimsy" made by the Iroquois Indians who lived near Niagara Falls. Let's hope they cherish our beadwork as much as we do.

Tools and Techniques

SOME BACKGROUND ON SEED BEADS

When you work with these tiny beads, you join a five-hundred-year tradition that spans most continents and even more cultures. Seed beads have been produced in Italy and the Czech Republic (formerly Czechoslovakia), also known as Bohemia, for hundreds of years. Glass seed beads, sometimes referred to by their French name, rocaille, are made by the *drawn* method of working glass, one of five methods that also include blowing, molding, winding (lampwork), and fusing. The drawn method involves taking a molten glob of glass, into which a bubble of air has been blown, and pulling it into a long hollow tube, usually about three hundred feet long! The air bubble becomes the hole in the bead. The tube is cut into pieces that become the seed beads or bugle beads. Seed beads are then heated and tumbled with clay-like material to slightly melt and round off the sharp edges. Further shaking after the beads cool causes the clay to fall out.

Finally, the beads are sorted by size. Because the holes in bugle beads are long, the holes cannot be filled with clay to prevent collapse when they are heated. As a result, these beads are not tumbled and their edges are sharp. Be aware that they can cut your thread!

Glass beads are made from sand and metals. The addition of different metals results in different colors, such as cobalt (blue), copper (blue, red, pink, and brown), chromium (green), cadmium (yellow), silver (amber), manganese (violet and pink with a brownish tinge), selenium (red and orange), and gold (ruby red and pink). Adding fluorine, tin, or phosphate changes the transparency of glass to opaque or opalescent. A semi-transparent glass is known as "greasy" glass because it resembles petroleum jelly. Opalescent glass gets its pearly look from the addition of bone.

Various color effects can be achieved in a variety of ways. Finishes on the outside of the beads can change their color. Types of finishes include iridescent (sometimes called carnival, rainbow, or aurora borealis [AB]), luster, gold-washed, galvanized (metallic, a finish that may rub off), dyed (the color may change), and pearlized or ceylon (a whitish coating). The appearance can also be changed by applying paint or other finishes inside the bead hole. Examples are silver-lined, gold-lined, or color-lined beads. Unusual effects are achieved by applying paint inside colored transparent beads, such as a transparent blue glass lined with violet paint. Another effect on color results from use of satin glass (a striated finish). You can affect the color by mixing two or more colors of beads together or by using different colors of thread.

Shapes can vary as well. Beads may be round, cylindrical, square, hexagon, trianglular, or facetted. Beads cut from tubes without rounding are called two-cuts, beads with many facets are called three-cuts and beads with only one facet are called charlottes. Charlottes are highly prized by some because they are somewhat hard to find and because they give a very subtle sparkle to your work.

Beads may be sold strung in hanks or by weight in tubes or bags. Japanese beads and

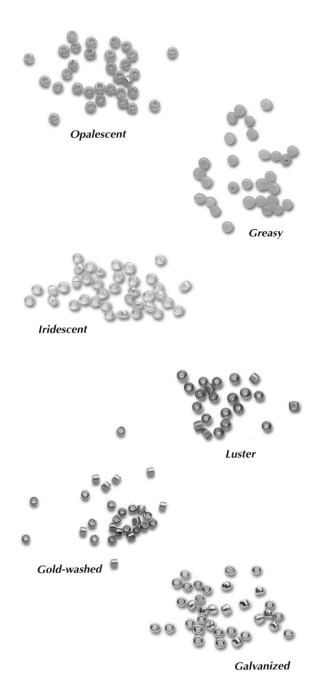

Opalescent

Greasy

Iridescent

Luster

Gold-washed

Galvanized

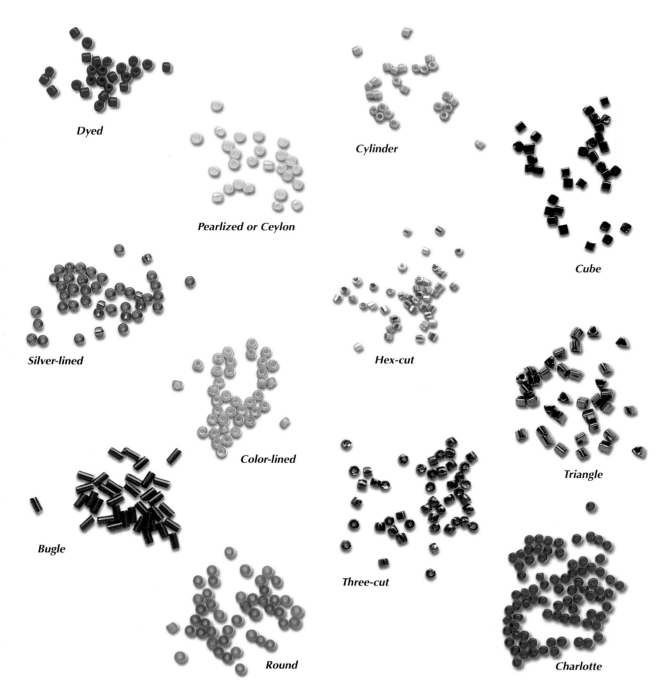

Dyed

Cylinder

Cube

Pearlized or Ceylon

Silver-lined

Hex-cut

Color-lined

Triangle

Bugle

Three-cut

Round

Charlotte

IN THE EARLY 1990S, seed beads were still made in seven countries. The Czech Republic led in output with 2,300 tons per year and the tiniest beads, 1.2 mm. India and Taiwan were the next largest producers at 1,400 tons each per year. Japan followed with 1,200 tons, Italy made 920 tons, France made 120 tons, and last, Austria with 80 tons. (Newsletter of the Bead Society of Greater Washington, Feb./Mar. 1990)

a wide range of actual sizes of beads within one size, depending on the manufacturer or country of origin. Japanese beads seem to be the most uniform and consistent in size. As in most projects, try to obtain all the beads needed for one project before you start, to ensure bead consistency.

BASIC BEADWORK TOOLS

The tools described below will help you get started with brick stitch. I keep my tools in a plastic pencil box and the lid serves as a work area when I am traveling. Inside the lid I have a magnetic strip to hold needles when I am working.

other non-European seed beads are usually sold by the gram or kilo, while Czech beads are most often sold strung in hanks. A hank consists of ten to fourteen strands, each twelve to fourteen inches in length. (Older hanks of beads may be only four to six inches in length.) One hank is approximately an ounce. Buying beads by weight may result in a differing number of beads per ounce because the size of the hole may vary, thus affecting the weight of the beads.

Bead sizes generally range from size 5 to size 18, but at one time they were made as small as size 24. The higher the number the smaller the bead. Sizes of beads are noted as 11° or simply size 11. This is read as "eleven/ought", "size eleven," or simply "elevens."

The most common bead size used today is size 11°, although new supplies of size 14/15 beads from Japan may make this size nearly as popular. Like shoes, there may be

- small sharp scissors
- several needles in a needle holder
- bobbins of Nymo D thread in several colors
- fresh clear nail polish (for coating knots)
- lighter (for melting knots and singeing short bits of thread on finished beadwork)
- 6-inch ruler
- beeswax
- small dishes or trays
- curved tweezers with a fine point for knotting and removing knots
- hemostat (a tool for gripping a needle to pull it through a tight bead or tight spot in the work. It opens or locks closed somewhat like scissors.)

Needles

Most beading needles are made in England or Japan. In English sizes, size 15 is the smallest and in Japanese, size 16 is the largest. The Japanese needles are very stiff while the English needles will bend rather than break. For most off-loom work where I pick up only one or a few beads at a time, I prefer the size 12 English needles, which are called "sharps." These needles are about 1¼ inches long. They are less expensive and bend less easily than beading needles. Size 12 sharps needles will go through most beads as small as size 14 or 15, depending on the size of thread used and the beads. Nymo D thread (see below) will go through a size 12 needle. I reserve English beading needles for loomwork or stringing long strands of beads. Use whichever needles you are comfortable with.

Threading a Needle

Always cut the thread at an angle with a small, sharp scissor so it will pass through the eye of the needle easily. Moisten your thread, then flatten it between your thumb and fingernail. Hold the thread between your thumb and forefinger and, with only about ¼ inch exposed, slide the thread into the eye of the needle. I hold the needle against a white surface so that it is easier to see the eye. Some people prefer to put the needle on the thread. Either way works.

Thread

My favorite thread, Nymo D, is made by the Belding-Hemmingway Company of Hender-sonville, North Carolina, which has been making thread for more than 150 years. It is a monocord nylon thread, which means it is made of several monofilaments similar to dental floss. It is very tough and durable. It is available on a bobbin that usually has eighty yards or on a spool that has about three hundred yards. Bobbins are now available in a variety of colors while the spools are generally available in only black or white. If you're really into beading, get a cone, which has more than four times the thread as a spool, and you'll be set with a near-lifetime supply.

I use Nymo thread for beadwork in several weights: D is the heaviest, B is medium, and A or 00 is the finest. Sizes F and G are also available and are heavier than D, but I seldom use them because they are too thick when multiple strands must fit in a bead hole.

If you compare Nymo D on the spool and on the bobbin, you'll notice a difference: The thread on a bobbin is softer and thinner than the thread on a spool, yet they are both marked D! To clear up this mystery a few years ago, I had a long conversation with a technician at the Belding Company who told me why. It has to do with the purpose for which this thread is manufactured: the shoe and leather industry. Shoes and purses are assembled on sewing machines that have a spool to feed thread to the needle and a bobbin to feed thread up from the bottom. The Nymo thread on the spool is made to feed the needle and so it is called a "needle" thread. Because it feeds through several tension mechanisms to the needle, it must be slightly stronger and is given a silicon coating to lubricate it as it passes through them. It is also bonded (heat-set) more tightly. The thread on bobbins is somewhat lighter weight and is coated with a slightly tacky adhesive to keep it from unraveling from the bobbin. Because it is bonded less tightly than spool thread, it may tend to flatten out more.

WEIGHT OR TENSILE STRENGTH OF NYMO THREAD

(breaking point when weight in pounds is placed on the thread)

	Spool thread	Bobbin thread
D	8.2	5.7
B	4.5	4.2
A	4.1	4.0
00	2.2	2.1

The bottom line is, if you want a softer feel to your beadwork, use the lighter weight thread that comes on the bobbin and don't pull your thread too tightly. If you want durability and a slightly stiffer feel to your work, use the heavier weight thread on the spool.

An alternative to Nymo thread is Silamide, size A, made by the A. H. Rice Company of Pittsfield, Massachusetts. It is a thread made for tailors and is available in a range of colors. Since it is a twisted thread, it may be a little more difficult to thread into the needle.

Beeswax

I wax my thread only for certain techniques, such as when I want two strands to stick together as one or when I want the wax to hold the beads in place for tight tension and stiff beadwork. Use fresh beeswax or micro-crystaline wax, which stays softer longer, for best results. Most wax sold for hand sewing is not as sticky as beeswax and is thus not as effective.

Thread Tension

Develop your ability to control your thread tension. When you want tight tension, wax your thread heavily, use thread heavy enough to fill the bead hole, and *pull tight*! If you want a soft, drapey feel to your beadwork, use a single thread and relax as you work, pulling gently on the thread.

Light Up Your Life

Good light is an absolute must when doing beadwork, especially as you get older. If you can't see the beads, the bead holes, and the needle eye, you just may need a little help. You may need to have your eyes checked or try the half-glasses that sit on the end of your nose for reading. A magnifying glass that rests on your chest and is supported by a cord can also be a big help. Special lamps that have a circular fluorescent bulb or incandescent bulb and a magnifying glass are great. A lamp may be freestanding or clamp-on and have a flexible arm so you can put it exactly where you need it. Recently, Ott Lites have become popular because they give light that distorts your bead colors less than other light.

I also rely on overhead or ambient light. Bouncing the light from the new halogen floor lamps off the ceiling can light a room up like daylight. Remember, the type of light used will affect how you see the color of your beads. I prefer an incandescent light over my left shoulder when I bead on the sofa.

BRICK STITCH TECHNIQUES

To get under way with brick stitch, work through the basics as shown in this section. With these techniques in your repertoire, you'll be amazed at what you can do.

Brick Stitch Base Row

There are many ways to do a base row for brick stitch; three methods are illustrated here. You may use the one you prefer, or the one that works best for your design. You may also substitute the edge of fabric or a fold in fabric for the base row. Please note that in brick stitch, each row added may be one or more beads tall. For this reason, the instructions will refer to adding "stacks" of beads to a row—a stack can have one or more beads in it. In the illustrations, a bold line indicates the new thread path.

Method One: Single-Needle Ladder

Thread a needle with 1½ yards of thread. For this first method we will use a stack that is only one bead tall, but you may use this method with bead stacks of any number of beads.

Step One: String on two stacks, form a loop, and tie the thread into a knot, leaving a 4" tail.

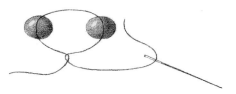

Step Two: Holding on to the tail with the knot at the bottom, go up through the stack on the right.

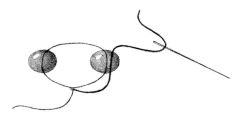

Stack A unit of beads used to work a row of brick stitch. A stack may be one or more beads tall.
Loop The thread bridge between two stacks of beads.

Step Three: Add one stack. Go up through the stack to the left, then down through the new stack just added.

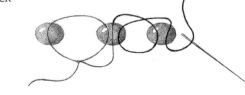

Step Four: Add a stack, go down through the previous stack and up through the new stack.

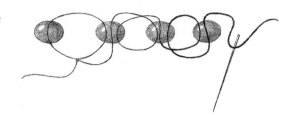

You now have four stacks connected and your thread is coming out of the top of the fourth stack (opposite the side where the tail is). Continue in this manner, repeating Steps Three and Four, adding stacks to make the base row as long as you wish.

Another way to describe this method is to add a stack, go through the previous stack from the end opposite where your thread is coming out, then through the new stack.

Method Two: Back Stitch

In this method, we will make a base row with stacks three beads tall but you may use this method for stacks of any height.

Thread a needle with 1½ yards of thread. Wrap the tail around your left forefinger three or four times. (If you're left-handed, wrap the thread around your right forefinger.)

Step One: String on enough stacks for your base row, in this case a multiple of three.

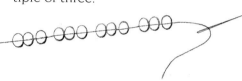

Step Two: Go through the second-to-last stack, working from the far end back. If your stacks are three beads tall, you go through the sixth, fifth, and fourth beads from the end.

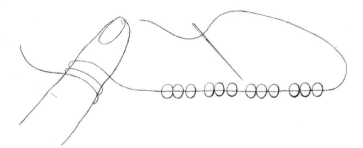

Step Three: Pull beads up tight so the two stacks lie next to each other.

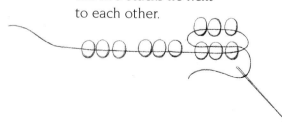

Step Four: Go through the next stack, again working from the far end, and pull the stack into place.

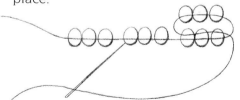

When all the beads are lying in stacks next to each other, knot the thread around the last loop to secure the base, then continue with the same thread. Leave the beginning tail to be woven in later.

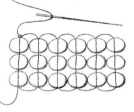

Method Three: Double-Row Base

This method of making a base row is similar to peyote stitch. It is an efficient way to start brick stitch because you are doing the first two rows at the same time. The instructions are given for single-bead stacks.

Step One: Thread a needle with 1½ yards of thread. String on three beads (stacks), leaving a 4" tail to be woven in later.

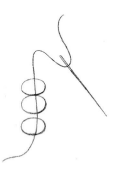

Step Two: Go back through the first stack.

Step Three: Position the stacks so they form a **T** and tie the working thread to the tail.

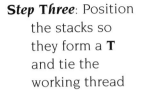

Step Four: Add one stack and go through the third stack added in Step One.

Step Five: Add one stack and go back through the stack added in the previous step.

Continue adding one stack and going back through the stack added in the previous step, repeating Steps Four and Five.

Flat Brick Stitch

Now that you've formed a base row, you're ready to proceed with the stitch. To begin a new row, you need to have the thread coming out of the top of the base row. If you've ended your base row with the thread coming out of the bottom, simply flip the beads over. If you've tied off your thread at the end of your base row, anchor a new thread in the base row and weave through the row until the thread is coming out of the top of an end bead.

Some people, like me, find it easier to always stitch in the same direction, for instance from left to right, which requires turning the work around at the end of each row. Others prefer to work back and forth, right to left, then left to right, always keeping the same side facing them. Choose whichever method you're comfortable with. Most illustrations in this book show the rows worked from left to right.

In order to keep a consistent number of stacks in each row, and to avoid an unsightly loop of thread outside the first stack, *a new row in brick stitch always begins with two stacks*.

Step One: With thread coming out of the top of a base row, add two stacks and catch the first exposed loop (the loop that's between the first and second stacks of the row below).

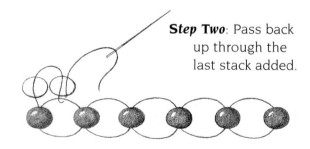

Step Two: Pass back up through the last stack added.

Step Three: Continue the row by adding one stack, catching the next loop, and passing back up through the last stack added.

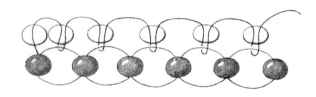

Decreasing

To add shaping to brick stitch beadwork, you may decrease at the beginning of a row or within a row.

Decreasing at the Beginning of a Row

To decrease at the beginning of a row, add two stacks and catch the *second* loop instead of the first one. To make the beads stand straight, a decrease stitch at the beginning of the row must be locked in using one of two methods.

Method One: Simple Lock Stitch

This method is illustrated for working single-bead stacks.

Step One: Add two stacks and catch the second loop of the row below.

Step Two: After coming back up through the second stack, go down through the first stack and up through the second stack again. See how the beads snap to attention!

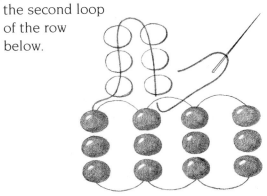

Method Two: Locking in the Row Below

This method is illustrated for working three-bead stacks.

Step One: Add two stacks and catch the second loop of the row below.

Step Two: Come back up through the second stack as usual.

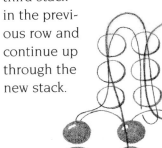

Step Three: Go down through the first stack, then down through the second stack of the previous row. Now go up through the third stack in the previous row and continue up through the new stack.

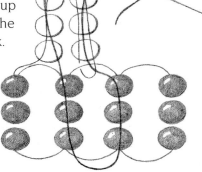

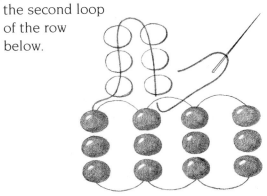

Decreasing Within a Row
Method One: Skipped-Loop Decrease

This method is illustrated for working rows of three-bead stacks.

Simply skip one loop when adding the next stack.

Method Two: Shared-Bead Decrease

Using the Skipped-Loop Decrease described above sometimes creates a hole in the beadwork, especially when working with stacks of two or more beads. To prevent this, use the Shared-Bead Decrease.

Step One: Add a stack and catch the next loop as usual, but when coming back up through the stack, do not go through the top bead.

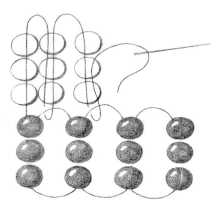

Step Two: Add another stack that is one bead less than the last one. Catch the next loop and come back up through the stack just added, plus the top bead from the previous stack. The top bead is now shared between two stacks.

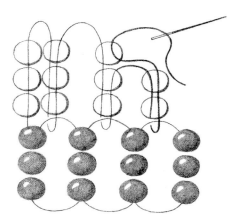

Increasing

Another way to add shaping to your beadwork is by increasing at the end of a row or within a row.

Increasing at the End of a Row
Method One: Ending Edge Increase

This method is illustrated for working rows of three-bead stacks.

Squeeze two stacks into the last loop, adding one stack at a time.

Step One: With the thread coming out of the last bead added, add one more stack and come up through the last stack again. Then go down through the new stack.

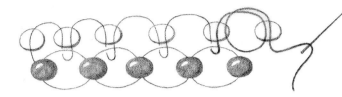

Step Two: Add one stack, go down through the previous stack and up through the new stack.

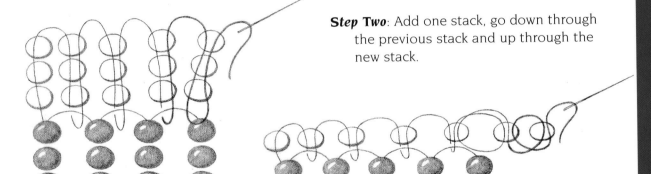

Method Two: Ending Edge Extension

This technique makes a large increase that extends out from the edge of the beadwork. You work as you do when making a base row. This method is illustrated for working single-bead stacks.

If the edge extension requires an odd number of stacks, first do an Ending Edge Increase, then continue as above repeating Steps One and Two until you've increased to the desired number of stacks. This will ensure that your thread ends up on top, ready to begin the next row.

Increasing Within a Row
Method One: Shared-Loop Increase

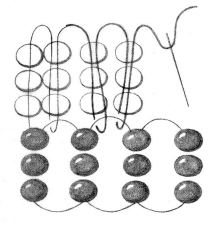

This method is illustrated for working rows of three-bead stacks.

Connect two or more stacks to any loop. When you're going to work this increase, a somewhat looser tension in the row below may be necessary to allow the stacks to fit in.

Method Two: Shared-Bead Increase

With stacks of two or more beads, the bottom bead may be shared between two stacks to reduce the number of beads and to allow your work to flare or ruffle.

Step One: Work the first stack of the increase in the usual way (plain brick stitch).

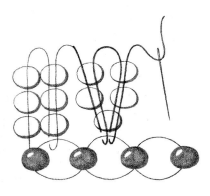

Step Two: Add a second stack with one less bead than the previous stack, go down through the bottom bead of the previous stack, catch the loop, and go back up through the whole stack.

Circular or Tubular Brick Stitch

Circular or tubular brick stitch may be used to create long chains or to cover an irregular shape. It may be done in one of two ways, either by working in a continuous spiral or by working level rows, one row on top of the previous row. Begin either method by making a base row in one of the ways shown on pages 32–35.

Method One: Continuous Spiral

This method is illustrated for working single-bead stacks.

Step One: With the thread coming out of the bottom of the second-to-last bead, position the last stack added on top of the second stack from the beginning.

Step Two: Pass the thread down through the first stack and up through the second stack and continue through the last stack added.

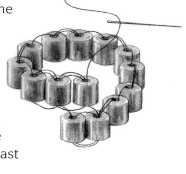

Step Three: Continue with brick stitch, adding one stack and catching the next loop, until your piece is as long as you want it.

Method Two: Level Rows

This method is illustrated for working single-bead stacks.

Step One: With the thread coming out of the top of the last stack, join the two ends by going down through the first stack and up through the last stack. If your thread is coming out of the bottom of the last bead, go up through the first stack and down through the last stack, then up through the next stack.

Step Two: Begin the next row by adding two stacks, catching the next loop, and passing back up through the last stack added.

Step Three: Continue around the row, adding one stack, catching the next loop, and passing back up through the last stack added.

Step Four: At the end of the row, pass down through the first stack of the row and back up through the last stack added.

Adding New Thread

When you have about 4 inches of thread left, it's time to add new thread. Leave the needle on the thread. Thread a new needle and knot the end with an overhand knot. Clip the tail close to the knot and singe it with a lighter or dab with clear nail polish. Bring the needle through three or four beads of the existing work so that the thread comes out of the same bead hole as the old thread and in the same direction. The knot will be buried inside the first bead and won't show.

Tie the old thread to the new thread with a square knot and dab with clear nail polish. Bring the old thread (with the needle still on it) through three to four beads and clip close to the beads. You're all set to keep beading with the new thread!

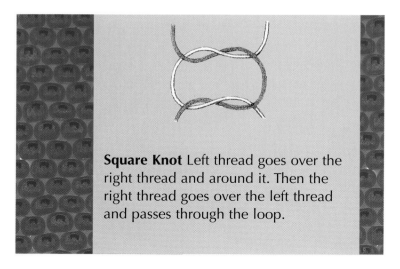

Square Knot Left thread goes over the right thread and around it. Then the right thread goes over the left thread and passes through the loop.

Weaving in Tails

To weave in beginning and ending tails, simply run your thread through four to six beads, then clip the thread close to the last bead.

Correcting Mistakes

As with most other forms of beadwork, the only way to correct most mistakes is by undoing the work back to the mistake and reworking. Brick stitch is a very tight stitch and difficult to take out. I remove my needle from the work and use the eye end of the needle to pull up on the loop between the last two beads.

Overhand knot

Finishing Brick Stitch Edges

Single-Bead Edge

The simplest way to cover the thread loops on the edge of brick stitch is to whip stitch or overcast stitch a bead along the edge. Anchor your thread so it is coming out of an end bead. Pick up a bead and catch the next loop. Do not go back up through the bead as you do in brick stitch; simply pick up another bead and go through the next loop. Continue across the edge adding two beads, one at a time, in the last loop.

Two-Bead Edge

Anchor your thread so it is coming out of an end bead. Add three beads. *Catch the next loop and pass back through last bead. Add two beads. Repeat from * across the edge.

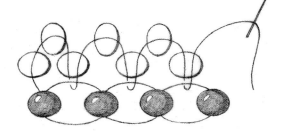

Triangle Edge

Anchor your thread so it is coming out of an end bead. Add three beads, catch the second loop, and pass back through only the last two beads. *Add three beads, catch the next loop, and pass back through the three beads added. Add four beads, catch the next loop, and pass back through the four beads added. Add three beads, catch the next loop, and pass back through the three beads added. Add two beads, catch the next loop, and pass back through the two beads added. Add one bead, catch the next loop, and pass back through the bead added. Add two beads, catch the next loop, and pass back through the two beads added. Repeat from *, adding one more bead each time up to four then one less down to one.

Bubble Edge

Anchor your thread so it is coming out of an end bead. Add one larger bead (for example, a size 8 or 6 seed bead) and one seed bead and pass back through the larger bead. Go down through the next bead in the base and up through the one next to it. Space according to the size of your beads.

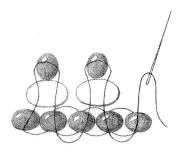

Spiky Edge

Anchor your thread so it is coming out of an end bead. Add one larger bead (for example, a size 8 or 6 seed bead). Add seed beads to desired length of first spike. Pass back through all beads except the tip bead, through the larger bead, and catch the thread loop. Pass through the larger bead again and make one or more additional spike(s). To begin the next spike, stitch down through the next bead in the base and come up through the one next to it.

Picot Edge

Anchor your thread so it is coming out of an end bead. Add four beads. *Pass back through second-to-last bead. Add two beads and catch second loop. Pass back through last bead. Add three beads. Repeat from * across the edge.

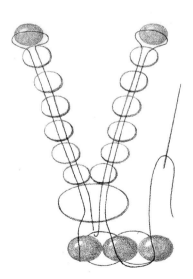

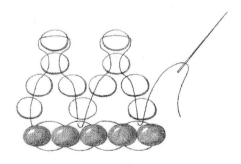

Two-Color Scalloped Edge

Anchor your thread so that it comes out the top of third bead from the left edge of the base.

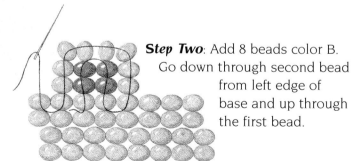

Step One: Add 4 beads color A. Go down through next bead in base and up through the next bead after that.

Step Two: Add 8 beads color B. Go down through second bead from left edge of base and up through the first bead.

Step Three: Add 12 beads color A. Go down through the sixth bead from left edge of base and up through the next bead to the right. Go down through the next bead and up through the next after that.

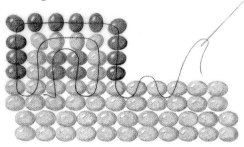

Step Four: Add 4 beads color A. Go down through next bead in base and up through the next bead after that.

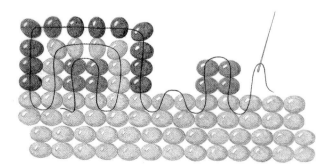

Repeat Steps Two through Four.

Working With Patterns

Working brick stitch in a pattern opens endless possibilities for all types of designs. Following a brick stitch pattern is easy. Unlike peyote stitch, where each row on the horizontal plane is offset from its neighbors, the rows in brick stitch are level. If you don't have access to a computer with a program for making charted patterns, it is easy to make your own with one of the grids included in this book. Three grids are provided: one-bead stack, two-bead stack, and three-bead stack. You can also make your own grid with stack heights that vary from row to row. Work with pencil and eraser at first so that it will be easy to fix the chart when you change your mind. Then color in your design with colored pencils or pens, or use symbols to represent a color.

Another way to create a pattern is to make a transparency of the grid you wish to use, then lay it over a colored picture or photo-graph and make a color photocopy of both pieces together. Because curved lines don't exactly follow the grid lines, you will have to decide which color to use in blocks that show one or more colors.

You may also wish to look for needlepoint design books for inspiration. Occasionally, you will find books such as *Designs and Patterns from North African Carpets and Textiles* by Jacques Revault (New York: Dover Publications, Inc., 1973) or *Authentic Algerian Carpet Designs and Motifs* by June Beveridge (New York: Dover Publications, Inc., 1978) which have beautiful charted patterns that may be used for brick stitch. And, in addition to the pattern books listed in the bibliography, there are more and more books coming on the market with brick stitch designs.

Explore this aspect of brick stitch and you will be amply rewarded.

Brick Stitch Grid. 1-bead stacks

Brick Stitch Grid. 2-bead stacks

Projects

Paisley Necklace

Egyptian Amulet Purse

Free-Form Bracelet

Diagonal Brick Stitch

O nce you've learned the basic technique of diagonal brick stitch, you can create many interesting variations. Basic Diagonal Brick Stitch is worked like regular brick stitch, but a pattern of decreases and increases at the edges of each row create the diagonal stair-step effect as illustrated below. Many different kinds of beads including cylinder beads, hex or triangle beads, and seed beads of all sizes can be used for this simple stitch.

Techniques

To increase at the beginning of a row, pick up two beads and catch the first loop.

To increase at the end of a row, work two beads, one at a time, into the last loop.

To decrease at the beginning of a row, pick up two beads and catch the second loop. When decreasing, always be sure to lock the stitch (see page 37).

Basic Diagonal Brick Stitch Bracelet

Begin with 1½ yd of single thread in a needle.

Row 1 (*base row*): Make a brick stitch base 6 beads wide using Method One, described on pages 32–33. Leave a 4" tail to be woven in later.

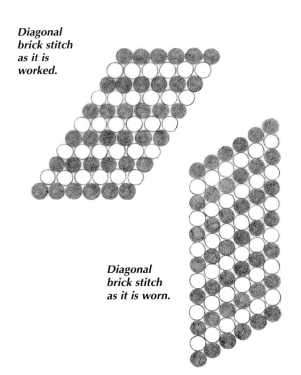

Diagonal brick stitch as it is worked.

Diagonal brick stitch as it is worn.

53

Row 2: Pick up two beads. Catch the first loop and go back up through the last bead. Work four more brick stitches across the row, one in each loop. You should have six beads in the row.

Peggy Wright

Row 3: Pick up two beads. Catch the second loop and go back up through the last bead. Lock the stitch. Work three more brick stitches across the row, one in each loop. Increase one in the last loop.

Liana Magee

NancyLee Dahlin

Repeat Rows 2 and 3 for desired length of bracelet or choker. For a closure, sew a button on one end and a loop of beads on the opposite end.

Overlapping Diamonds Bracelet

The pink and black diamonds bracelet shown here uses size 8 hex beads. The diamonds are seven beads wide and six rows tall.

Begin with about 1 yd of single thread in a needle.

Row 1 (*base row*): Make a brick stitch base 7 beads wide using Method One (see pages 32–33). Leave a 4" tail to be woven in later.

Row 2: Pick up two beads. Catch the second loop and go back through the last bead. Lock the stitch. Work 1 brick stitch in each loop across the row. Increase one in the last loop. (See Row 3, page 54.)

Row 3: Pick up two beads. Catch the first loop and go back up through the last bead. Work 5 more brick stitches across the row.

Repeat Rows 2 and 3 once, then Row 2 once more. Leave the thread tails and use them later to sew the diamonds together.

Make enough diamonds in two or more

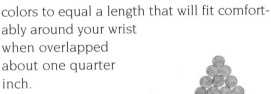

colors to equal a length that will fit comfortably around your wrist when overlapped about one quarter inch.

Join the Diamonds

Think of the diamonds as little bits of fabric. To sew them together, position one on top of the other and hold firmly in place. With thread anchored in one diamond, push the needle down between the beads nearest where your thread is exiting a bead. Go through one or two beads in the bottom diamond, then up between the beads to the top diamond. Go through one or two beads, then down between the beads again to the bottom. Continue to sew in this manner until the diamonds are securely joined.

Closure

One of my favorite closures for beadwork is a simple clothing snap. The diamonds are continuous and there is no gap for an ordinary clasp. Sew on a snap in the same way you sewed the diamonds together.

Diamond Sautoir

To make the necklace shown here, use size 10 triangle beads with one 6 mm bead between each diamond. Begin with about 2 yd of thread and use it double.

Begin by tying one side of a clasp to the end of your thread. You may use your favorite clasp—a lobster clasp is shown here. Add one 6 mm bead.

Continue as usual until there are 5 beads in the base row.

Row 2: Pick up 2 beads, catch the *first* loop and go back up through the last bead. Work 3 more brick stitches across the row.

Row 3: Pick up 2 beads, catch the *second* loop and go back up through the last bead. Lock the stitch. Work 2 more brick stitches. Increase 1 bead in last loop.

Row 4: Repeat Row 2.

Row 5: Repeat Row 3.

After completing a diamond, add a 6 mm bead and repeat Rows 1–5. Continue in this manner, working with the same thread and adding new thread only when necessary. When the necklace is the desired length, and ending with a 6 mm bead, add the other half of the clasp to the end, knot the thread, and weave in the tails.

Row 1: Make a brick stitch base 5 beads wide using Method One (pages 32–33). Be sure to keep the first bead snug up against the 6 mm bead. Go down through the second bead added.

Zigzag Bracelet

By changing the pattern of increases and decreases in the Basic Diagonal Brick Stitch, different shapes can be made. Here we'll do a variation that will look like a zigzag and may remind some of rickrack. For this pattern, we'll work rows from left to right and from right to left—the arrows after the row numbers indicate the direction in which the row is worked.

Row 1 → : Make a base row 5 beads wide using Method One (see pages 32–33).

Row 2 ← : Pick up 2 beads, catch the second loop, and go back up through the last bead. Lock the stitch. Work 2 brick stitches. Increase one bead in last loop.

Row 3 → : Pick up 2 beads, catch the first loop, and go back up through the last bead. Work 3 brick stitches.

Row 4 ← : Repeat Row 2.

Row 5 → : Repeat Row 3.

Row 6 ← : Pick up 2 beads, catch the first loop, and go back up through the last bead. Work 3 brick stitches.

Row 7 → : Pick up 2 beads, catch the second loop, and go back up through the last bead. Lock the stitch. Work 2 brick stitches. Increase one bead in last loop.

Row 8 ← : Repeat Row 6.

Row 9 → : Repeat Row 7.

Repeat Rows 2 through 9 for desired length. For a closure, use the snap method described for the Overlapping Diamonds Bracelet. For another variation, make the first and last beads of each row a contrasting color.

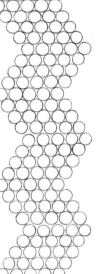

Petroglyph Necklace

This necklace is a typical style made by Zulu women of South Africa. It is composed of eleven triangles that are connected to a base row and separated by swags of beads. I've changed the pattern slightly by adding a petroglyph motif to each triangle. You may make a necklace using the petroglyph patterns provided or use the blank triangles to do your own design which may be geometric, floral, your initials, or whatever you like. The necklace is worked in rows along the entire length of the piece rather than by making individual triangles and adding swags later. Look for uniform beads so that your swags will hang evenly.

Note: *Depending on the size of your beads, you may need to adjust the number of beads in the swags between the triangles. Lay the necklace in a circle or try it on to see if the swags are draping okay. Add or subtract beads as necessary.*

Supplies

Size 11° seed beads: Dark background color (D), 1½ ounces; light accent color (L), ⅔ ounce.
Nymo D thread, one bobbin to match beads.

Abbreviations

BT (Back Through) Pass the needle through the bead in the opposite direction of the last pass through the bead, i.e., toward the tail.

The Base Band

The base band is made of two rows. The top row is 2 beads tall and there are 194 beads across. The bottom row is 1 bead tall and 193 beads across with 192 loops across the bottom. Leave a tail of thread to indicate the left

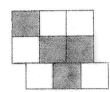

The bottom row of the base is one bead tall and the top row is 2 beads tall.

side of your work. Work the pattern shown above and described below, or make the band all one color. Begin with 1½ yd of single thread.

Making the Band

A. String on five beads: 2L, 1D, 1L, 1D. BT first L. Knot tail to working thread.
B. Add 1D, BT 1D and 1L.
C. Add 1L and 1D, BT 1D.

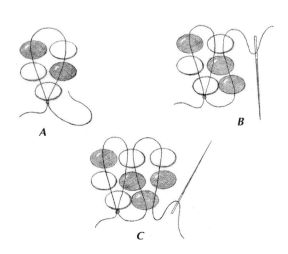

A

B

C

D. Add 1L, BT 1D and 1L.
E. Add 1D and 1L, BT 1L.
F. Add 1L, BT 1L and 1D.
G. Add 1L and 1D, BT 1L. Repeat from B to G.

Triangles and Swags

Note: *At the beginning of each row, catch the second loop and lock the stitch by going forward through all six beads again.*

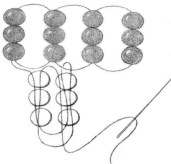

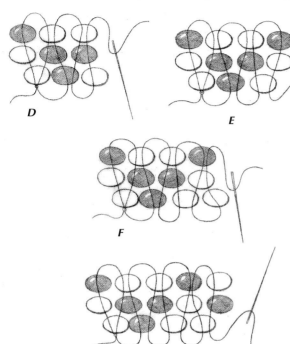

D

E

F

G

Row 1: Continuing with the same thread and following the chart on page 65 from left to right, work 12 three-bead stacks.

Swag: Add 19 beads, alternating light and dark beads and beginning and ending with a light bead. Add the first three-bead

NancyLee Dahlin

stack of the next triangle and catch the seventh loop, counting from where you finished the last stitch.

Continue across the row following the pattern on page 65 and adding swags between each triangle. The numbers above each triangle indicate where that triangle is repeated within the necklace. For example, the first triangle is used in the first, sixth, and eleventh positions, the second triangle is in the second and seventh positions, and so on.

Row 2: Work the pattern in the opposite direction, that is from right to left. This time the triangles will have 11 stacks and swags will have 21 beads. Remember to catch the second loop and lock in the stitch (see page 60) at the beginning of the row. After adding swag beads, add the first three-bead stack for the next triangle and catch the first loop of the next triangle.

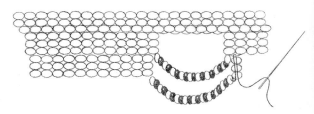

Row 3: Work the pattern from left to right. Each triangle will have 10 stacks and swags will have 23 beads. Remember to catch the second loop and lock the stitch (see page 60) at the beginning of the row.

Row 4: Work the pattern from right to left. Triangles have 9 stacks; swags have 25 beads.

Row 5: Work the pattern from left to right. Triangles have 8 stacks; swags have 27 beads.

Row 6: Work the pattern from right to left. Triangles have 7 stacks; swags have 31 beads.

Row 7: Work the pattern from left to right. Triangles have 6 stacks; swags have 37 beads. This is the last row that has swags.

Row 8: Triangles have 5 stacks, no swags. Complete each triangle separately, working Rows 9–11.

Row 9: Triangles have 4 stacks.

Row 10: Triangles have 3 stacks.

Row 11: Triangles have 2 stacks. As you are locking in the stitch, just after you've caught the loop and come back through the last three-bead stack, make a picot point as follows.

Peggy Wright

Carol Perkins

Picot Point

Add 4 beads, come back through the first of the four, then finish locking in the stitch. Tie off the thread and weave in the tail.

Finishing the Top Edge

This finishing edge looks like two rows of beads sitting on top of the beginning row and is worked somewhat like square stitch.

Anchor your thread so it is coming out of the top of the first bead of the top edge. Add three beads and catch the first loop.

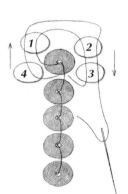

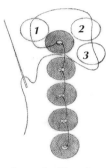

Shown looking down at the top edge.

Add one bead and go back through the first bead and forward through the second and third beads.

Add one bead, go under the loop, add one bead, back through the bead on the left, and forward through the last two beads on the right. Continue in this manner across the entire edge.

Making a Closure

Sew a bead or button to one end of the band. Anchor a thread in the other end of the band and make a beaded loop large enough to fit over the bead or button. To make the necklace adjustable, make two or three loops.

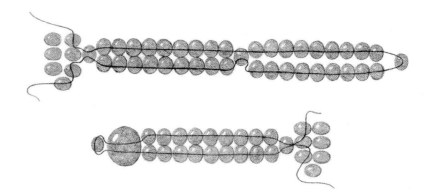

Option: Cover a 4 mm bead with matching seed beads by wrapping them around the bead and then through the hole. Every two rows of beads will share the first and last bead nearest the hole. Pass the needle through the hole and tie working thread to tail. *Add just enough seed beads to reach around half the bead, then pass the needle through the 4 mm bead again. Go through the first bead added. Now add the same number of beads again, less two, and go through the last bead of the previous group. Pass through the hole of the 4 mm bead. Repeat from * until bead is covered.

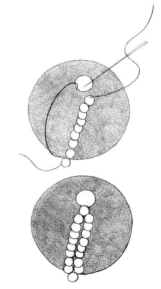

Petroglyph figures

1st, 6th, and 11th	2nd and 7th	3rd and 8th	4th and 9th	5th and 10th

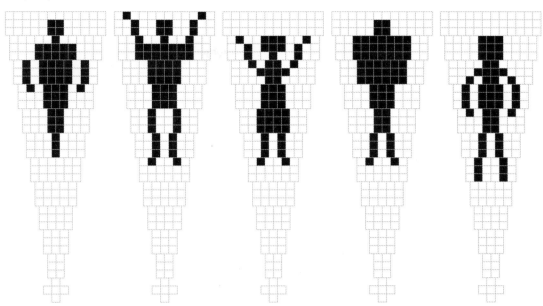

Design blanks

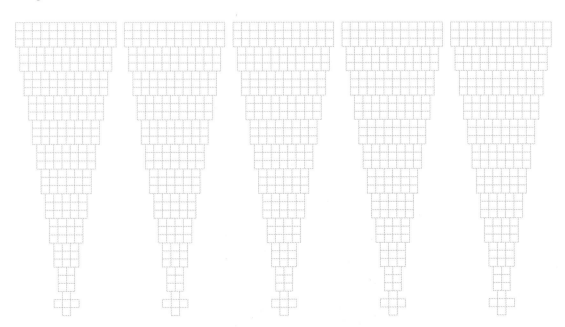

Sweet Little Bow Pin

This brick stitch pin is made of four individual parts that are joined together: two bow loops and two tails. The ones shown here use a combination of cylinder beads and seed beads, and results will vary if other beads are used. Combine opaque and silver-lined beads for a smart little bow. This project will give you practice in increasing, decreasing, and shaping with brick stitch.

Supplies

Cylinder beads (Delicas or Antiques), 5 grams
Size 11° seed beads, 3 grams
Pin back
Nymo D thread to match either bead

The following instructions apply throughout this project:

Abbreviations

Stack (stk) The number of beads in a column picked up for one stitch. A stack may have one or more beads.
Cylinder beads (cyl bd) Beads such as Delicas made by the Miyuki Company and Antiques made by the Toho Company.
Seed beads (sd bd) Round, size 11° seed beads.

Loop (lp) The thread bridge between two stacks of beads in a row.
Increase (inc) Add one extra stack of beads in the same loop so there are two stacks instead of one.
Decrease (dec) Decreasing is done in two ways: (1) Add no beads to a loop (skip a loop), thereby decreasing the number of beads in the row, and (2) Work a Shared-Bead Decrease (see page 38).

The strings of numbers indicate how many stacks are added in each loop across a row: 2, 1, 2, 0, 2 means that there are the usual two stacks in the first loop, one stack in the second loop, 2 stacks in the third loop (increase), no stack in the fourth loop (decrease) and so on.
The numbers in parentheses indicate how many stacks are added to that row. (8 sd bd stks) means you've added 8 stacks of 1 seed bead each; (12 cyl bd stks) means that you've added 12 stacks of 3 cylinder beads each.
Each row begins with 2 stacks, and you catch either the first or second loop as indicated. When you begin a row by catching the second loop,

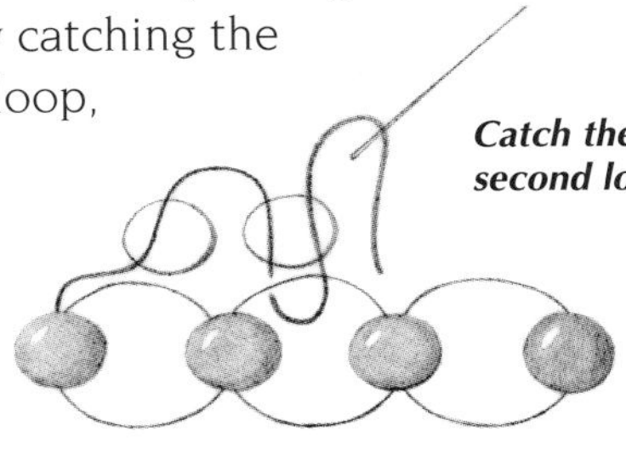

Catch the second loop.

67

always lock the stitch so the beads will lie properly. After catching the loop and

Lock the stitch.

coming back up through the second bead added, lock the stitch by going down through the first bead and up through the second bead.

Start each part with 1¾ yd of thread and use single throughout.

Check bead counts after every row and mark off rows as you finish them. There is always one less loop across the row than there are stacks.

Bow Loops (Make two)

For the bow loops, odd numbered rows are cylinder beads (cyl bd) and each stack (stk) is three beads tall. Even numbered rows are seed beads (sd bd) and each stack (stk) is one bead tall.

Row 1: Work a base row with 7 cyl bd stks across.

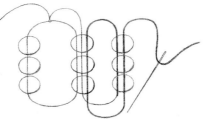

Work base row of 3-bead stacks . . .

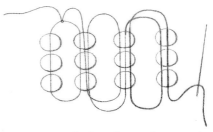

. . . until there are 7 stacks in the row.

Row 2: Catch first lp and inc in last lp. (8 sd bd stks)

Row 3: Catch first lp and inc as follows: 2, 1, 2, 2, 2, 1, 2. (12 cyl bd stks)

Row 4: Catch first lp and inc in last lp. (13 sd bd stks)

Row 5: Catch first lp and inc as follows: 2, 1, 2, 1, 2, 1, 1, 2, 1, 2, 1, 2. (18 cyl bd stks)

Row 6: Catch first lp and work even. (18 sd bd stks)

Row 7: Catch first lp and work even. (18 cyl bd stks)

Note: *The bow loop piece begins to curve now. Shape it over your finger and keep your tension tight!*

Row 8: Catch second lp and dec as follows: 0, 2, 1, 0, 1, 1, 1, 1, 0, 1, 1, 1, 1, 0, 1, 1, 1. (14 sd bd stks)

Row 9: Catch second lp, add 1 more stack (3 stacks are now in the row).

*Work a Shared Bead Decrease (^) as follows: Add 3 beads, catch the next loop, come up through 2 *beads only.*

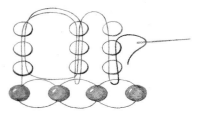

Work a 2-bead stack in the next loop and when you come back up, catch the third bead from the previous stack.

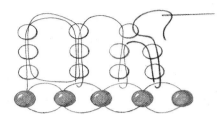

loop from beginning and ending edges. Go back up through second bead. Continue working in brick stitch across the row, catching beginning and ending edge loops with each stitch. (6 sd bds)

Row 17: Catch second loop. (5 stks of sd bds, each stk 2 bds tall)

When both bow loops are complete, butt the edges together and join by weaving back and forth through the edge beads.

Work 3 stacks as usual. Repeat from * once more. The complete row looks like this: 0, 2, 1, ^, 1, 1, 1, ^, 1, 1, 1 (11 cyl bd stks; Shared-Bead Decreases count as 1. ^ indicates a shared-bead decrease.)

Row 10: Catch second lp, work even. (10 sd bd stks)

Row 11: Catch first lp, work even. (10 cyl bd stks)

Row 12: Catch second lp, work even. (9 sd bd stks)

Row 13: Catch first lp, work even. (9 cyl bd stks)

Row 14: Catch second lp, work even. (8 sd bd stks)

Row 15: Catch second lp, work even. (7 cyl bd stks)

Row 16: Fold work in half. To join beginning and ending edges, catch first loop from beginning edge and first loop from last edge and knot thread. Pick up two seed beads and catch second

First Bow Tail

Leave an 8" tail with which to sew the bow tail to the bow loop.

Row 1: Work base row as shown for bow loops with 5 cyl bd stks.

Row 2: Catch first lp, work even. (5 sd bd stks)

Row 3: Catch first lp and inc as follows: 2, 2, 1, 2. (7 cyl bd stks)

Row 4: Catch second lp, work even. (6 sd bd stks)

Row 5: Catch first lp and inc as follows: 2, 1, 2, 1, 2. (8 cyl bd stks)

Row 6: Catch first lp, work even. (8 sd bd stks)

Doris Coghill

Row 7: Catch first lp and inc as follows: 2, 1, 2, 1, 2, 1, 2. (11 cyl bd stks)

Row 8: Catch second lp, work even. (10 sd bd stks)

Row 9: Catch first lp and inc as follows: 2, 1, 1, 1, 2, 1, 1, 1, 2. (12 cyl bd stks)

Row 10: Catch second lp, work even. (11 sd bd stks)

Picot Edge

Pick up 3 cyl bds, catch first lp, pass back up through last cyl bd added. *Pick up 1 cyl bd and make a brick st in next lp. Pick up 2 cyl bds, catch next lp, back up through last cyl bd added (picot).

Susan Manchester

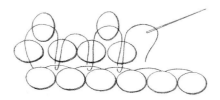

Repeat from * 4 times. Work 1 brick stitch and 1 picot in last lp. Tie off thread. Sew beginning edge of tail to bottom of the beads between the bow loops. Tie off thread.

Second Bow Tail

Leave an 8" tail to sew the bow tail to the bow loops. Work Rows 1 through 4 in seed bead stacks, then beginning with Row 5, alternate rows of cylinder bead stacks and seed bead stacks.

Row 1: Pick up 4 sd bds.
Go back through beads 2 and 1. Knot tail to thread.

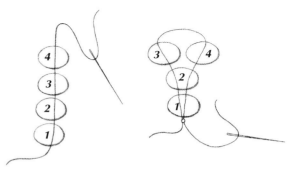

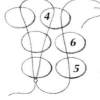

Add 2 sd bds and go back through bead 4.

Add 1 sd bd and go back through beads 6 and 5.

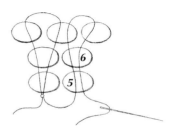

Continue until there are 4 beads across the top row and 3 stks of sd bds. Flip the piece over so the tail is at the top.

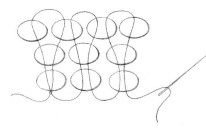

Row 2: Catch first lp and inc in last lp. (4 sd bds)

Row 3: Catch second lp, work in stks of 2 sd bds each. (3 sd bd stks)

Row 4: Catch first lp, inc in last lp. (4 sd bds)

Row 5: Cyl bd stks are 3 beads tall. Catch first lp and inc as follows: 2, 1, 2. (5 cyl bd stks)

Continue with Row 2 of the directions for the First Bow Tail and work through Row 10.

Finishing

Position the second tail so that it is on top of the first tail and the top edge is at the top of the area between the bow loops. Sew second bow tail to bow loops. Sew pin back to back of bow. Squish bow loops together slightly to make them poof up.

Peggy Wright

Victorian Tassel

Everyone loves tassels, but whether they have any practical use is questionable. It may be that their sole purpose is to delight the eye with their lavish color, shape, and movement. They beckon us to touch them. Victorian tassels graced four-poster beds, window draperies, and even birdcages. They may also have adorned a garment to enhance the status of the wearer. This brick stitch tassel design calls for bugle beads and three-cut seed beads, but you may also use cylinder beads to make a design in the square at the top.

Peggy Wright

Supplies

No. 2 bugle beads, ½ ounce
Size 9°, 10°, or 11° three-cut beads, ½ ounce
¾"-wide ribbon, 2 inches
Small piece of batting or other material for stuffing
No. 2 cork (color cork with a permanent marker to match beads and pierce through center with an awl)
Nymo D thread to match beads

Square for Tassel Top

Note: *The size of your finished "square" will depend on the size beads you're using. Rows 1 through 7 should have a finished measurement of approximately one inch.*

With brick stitch (see pages 32–36 for basic instructions), make a piece of beadwork two inches wide and with rows as follows:
Row 1: Three-cut beads
Rows 2 and 3: Bugle beads
Row 4: Three-cut beads
Rows 5 and 6: Bugle beads
Row 7: Three-cut beads
Fold this piece in half so you have an approximate one-inch square and stitch side beads together.

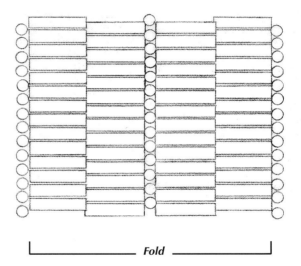

Fold

Ribbon Pillow Stuffing

Fold ribbon in half, stitch sides together, and insert small piece of stuffing so it is about ⅛" thick. Fold raw edges to the inside and sew edge closed.

73

Triangle Top

Work a brick stitch triangle along the folded edge of the ribbon pillow, decreasing at the beginning of each row (see pages 36–37) until there are two beads left. Add a loop of beads and go through it twice, ending by going back through the first bead of the loop and tying off the thread.

Insert the ribbon pillow into the beadwork square, keeping the beadwork triangle free and coming out of the top of the square, and close the beadwork square by weaving back and forth between beads.

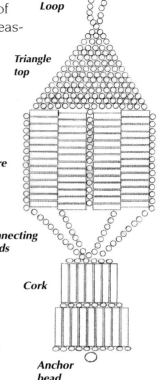

Loop

Triangle top

Square

Connecting beads

Cork

Anchor bead

Covering the Cork

With brick stitch (see pages 32–36 for basic instructions), make a piece of beadwork that will fit around the cork with rows as follows:

Row 1: Three-cut beads. This is the base row. Use the Single-Needle Ladder technique described on pages 32–33.

Jane Langenback

Carol Perkins

Row 2: Bugle beads.
Row 3: Three-cut beads.
Row 4: Bugle beads.
Row 5: Three-cut beads.

To shape the beadwork to fit the cork, increase one bead near the middle of each row. Sew the edges of the beadwork together so they fit tightly around the cork and glue the beadwork to the cork.

Add Fringe

String one strand of fringe from each bead along the lower edge of the cork as follows: String 2½" of three-cut beads, then 3" of bugle beads. Add 3 three-cut beads, then pass back through the strand and over to the next bead.

Attach the cork to the square with four strands of connecting beads as shown on page 74, going through the cork and through an anchor bead at the bottom of the cork.

Susan Manchester

Joanne Hite

Liana Magee

Crossroads Bracelet

U se the edge increasing and decreasing techniques from pages 36–37 and 39 to make this simple bracelet. Select two highly contrasting beads for this piece, such as matte and shiny or complementary colors. You may use any beads from size 11° to 8° in round seed beads, cylinder beads, hex beads, triangles, or cubes. Round beads will make smooth edges while cylinder beads make sharper zigzags. In

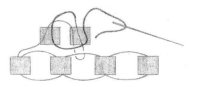

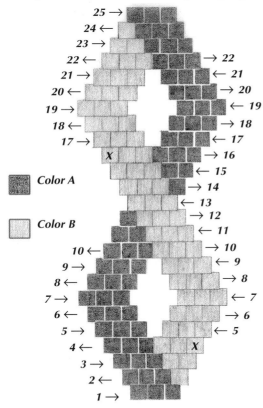

Abbreviations

lp = loop

lock st = anchor beads as for a beginning
edge decrease.

As with all brick stitch work, start each row with two beads. For example, Row 2 adds 1 B and 3 A beads—begin by working 1 B and 1 A, then add 2 more A beads, one at a time. Catch the first or second loop as indicated. If catching the second loop, lock the stitch as shown above. Work with a single thread.

Row 1 → : With color A, make a base row of
three beads (see pages 32–34).

Row 2 ← : Catch the first lp, 1 B and 3 A

Row 3 → : Catch the first lp, 3 A and 2 B

Row 4 ← : Catch the first lp, 3 B and 3 A

Work left side only

Row 5 → : Catch the first lp, 3 A

Row 6 ← : Catch the second lp (lock st) 3 A

Row 7 → : Catch the first lp, 3 A

Row 8 ← : Catch the first lp, 3 A

Row 9 → : Catch the second lp (lock st) 3 A

Row 10 ← : Catch the first lp, 3 A. Tie off
thread.

Anchor new thread coming up out of bead marked X in Row 4.

the figure, rows are numbered left and right, and an arrow indicates the direction the row is worked. For earrings, make half the pattern, then glue post or clip-on earring findings to the back. The amount of beads will vary depending on the size and length of the bracelet.

Liana Magee

Work right side only

Row 5 ← : Catch the first lp, 3 B
Row 6 → : Catch the second lp (lock st) 3 B
Row 7 ← : Catch the first lp, 3 B
Row 8 → : Catch the first lp, 3 B
Row 9 ← : Catch the second lp (lock st) 3 B
Row 10 → : Catch the first lp, 3 B
Row 11 ← : Catch the second lp, 2 B. Lock this stitch.

Join left and right sides of Row 10 as shown below, then work 1 B and 2 A.

Row 12 → : Catch the second lp (lock st) 1 A and 3 B
Row 13 ← : Catch the second lp (lock st) 3 B
Row 14 → : Catch the first lp, 3 B, 1 A

Row 15 ← : Catch the first lp, 2 A, 3 B
Row 16 → : Catch the first lp, 3 B, 3 A

Work right side only

Row 17 ← : Catch the first lp, 3 A
Row 18 → : Catch the second lp (lock st) 3 A
Row 19 ← : Catch the first lp, 3 A
Row 20 → : Catch the first lp, 3 A
Row 21 ← : Catch the second lp (lock st) 3 A
Row 22 → : Catch the first lp, 3 A. Tie off thread.

Anchor thread coming up out of bead marked X in Row 16.

Work left side only

Row 17 → : Catch the first lp, 3 B
Row 18 ← : Catch the second lp, (lock st) 3 B
Row 19 → : Catch the first lp, 3 B
Row 20 ← : Catch the first lp, 3 B
Row 21 → : Catch the second lp, (lock st) 3 B
Row 22 ← : Catch the first lp, 3 B
Row 23 → : Catch the second lp, 2 B (lock st).

Peggy Wright

Join right and left sides of Row 22 as shown below, then work 3 A.

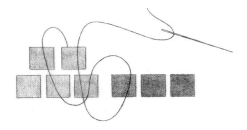

Row 24 ← : Catch the second lp (lock st), 3 A and 1 B

Row 25 → : Catch the second lp (lock st), 3 A
Repeat Rows 2-25 to desired length.

Add a pre-made closure or attach a loop to one end and a bead or button to the other. A clothing snap may also be used as a closure.

Alois Powers

Carol Perkins

Paisleys

The paisley motif derives its name from the town of Paisley, Scotland, where machine-woven woolen shawls were made to imitate the luxurious shawls imported from Kashmir, India in the nineteenth century. The pine cone or bent-teardrop design probably evolved from a motif called the *buti*, which means flower, favored by fifteenth century Moghuls and often used in Oriental rugs. This curvilinear form, used alone or in a grouping, has waxed and waned in popularity throughout the centuries, but has never completely disappeared. Brick stitch is the ideal stitch to make such a shape because its linear quality emphasizes the shape, curves, and slightly tilted tip. Imagine doing it in any other stitch and the results would not be as satisfying.

There are many ways to use beaded paisley shapes. A pair can be glued to earring findings. A single one can be a pin or a shoe clip. Several can be assembled into a necklace, purse decoration, or headband.

Supplies

One teardrop-shaped bead, 15 × 8 mm with lengthwise hole.

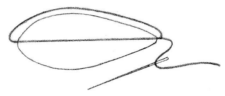

Size 11° seed beads: small amounts of related colors. A good combination could include one light, two medium, and one dark color. (Other sizes of beads may be used for various effects.)
Size 14° seed beads: enough for the edges

Step One: With a single thread, pass your needle through the teardrop bead and tie the working thread to the tail. Leave a 4" tail to be woven in later.

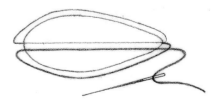

Pass the needle again through the teardrop bead, going from the wide end to the narrow end. You now have thread entirely encircling the bead. Tie the thread to the tail again to maintain tension.

Step Two: Pick up two beads and begin a brick stitch row around the teardrop bead, anchoring the stitches to the thread around the bead. Be sure the first bead is near the hole at the narrow end of the teardrop bead.

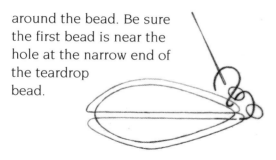

Step Three: Work single-bead brick stitch around the entire bead. The first and last bead should extend slightly from the tip of the teardrop bead.

Step Four: Add one bead (tip bead), pass through the first bead of the row from the outside toward the teardrop, then through the last bead of the row from the teardrop side toward the outside.

Step Five: Pass back through the tip bead. You are now ready to begin the next row the same way as the first.

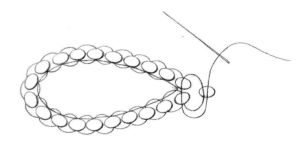

Step Six: Pick up two beads and catch the first loop next to where your thread exits the tip bead. Work brick stitch around, increasing so the work stays flat, and join the rows at the narrow end as described above.

Step Seven: To make the tail of the paisley curl, decrease one bead near the beginning of the third row (remembering to lock the stitch), continue around with brick stitch, increase one bead in the last loop, and join the rows as described above.

Note: *When decreasing for the curl, do not decrease at the very beginning of the row— wait until the second or third brick stitch. This will ensure that you have the beginning and ending bead in the right position for adding the next tip bead.*

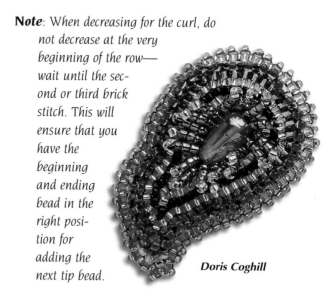

Doris Coghill

Picot Edge

With size 14° beads and single thread, anchor thread in tip bead and add four beads. *Pass back through the second-to-last bead. Add two beads, catch the third loop, and pass back through the last bead. Add three beads. Repeat from *, skipping one or two loops each time, depending on the curvature.

Note: *When working around the wide end of the paisley, you will have to increase in some places by not skipping any loops.*

Work completely around the paisley, ending in the last tip bead opposite your starting point. Make one more picot at the tip.

Joining the Paisleys

To sew two paisleys together, I treat them very much like two small pieces of fabric. They may be overlapped or joined edge to edge. To join them overlapping, position one paisley on top of the other and hold firmly in place. With the thread anchored in one paisley, push the needle down between the beads nearest where your thread is exiting a bead. Go through one or two beads in the bottom paisley, then up between the beads to the top. Go through one or two beads, then down between the beads again to the bottom. Continue in this manner until the paisleys are securely joined.

To join paisleys edge to edge, lay two paisleys next to each other so that they fit somewhat like puzzle pieces. With thread anchored in one paisley, weave back and forth through the edge beads. If paisleys don't exactly fit together, add a seed bead or two to fill the space.

Jane Langenback

Liana Magee

Joanne Hite

Peggy Wright

Telsem Necklace

M any cultures rely on beads worn or carried to remind them of religious or spiritual aspects of their lives. In Ethiopia, women wear beads called *telsem* that resemble tiny silver boxes strung on a heavy cord. The boxes may be shaped as rectangles, triangles, or semi-circles. This necklace, made with modern cylinder beads and Bali silver beads, reflects the overall look and feel of the traditional Ethiopian necklace.

Supplies

15 grams Toho Antiques #602 Galvanized
    Steel
5 grams Miyuki Delicas, #310 Matte Black
28 Bali silver rondelles, size 6 mm
14 round silver beads, size 3 mm
7 tubular silver beads, 10 mm long
34 round silver beads, size 6 mm
28 Bali silver beads, size 6 mm
Size 12 sharps needles
1 clasp (I used a barrel-type clasp here)
Nymo D thread in gray
1½ yd FF bead cord
2 bead tips
1 dental floss threader (used as a stringing
    device and available at most pharmacies)

With brick stitch (see pages 32–36 for basic instructions) and using Nymo thread, make seven pieces following the diagram and the written instructions. Use #602 Galvanized Steel for the light beads (A) and #310 Matte Black for the dark beads (B). When the instruction calls for catching the second loop,

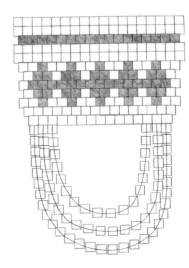

which means decreasing at the beginning of the row, be sure to lock the stitch as described on page 37.

Row 1: With color A, make a base row of 18 two-bead stacks using Method One or Two (see pages 32–34).

Row 2: Catch the second loop. Work a row of single-bead stacks in color B—17 beads added.

Row 3: Catch the first loop. Work a row of two-bead stacks in color A—18 stacks added, 2 stacks in last loop.

Note: *Stacks for all remaining rows are one-bead tall.*

Row 4: Catch the second loop. *Work 2A, 1B. Repeat from * across row, ending with 2A.

Row 5: Catch the second loop. *Work 1A, 2B. Repeat from * across row, ending with 1A.

Row 6: Catch the first loop. First and last

beads are color A, the rest are color B. Add 17 stacks total, with 2 stacks in the last loop.

Row 7: Catch the second loop. *Work 1A, 2B. Repeat from * across row, ending with 1A—16 stacks added.

Row 8: Catch the first loop. *Work 2A, 1B. Repeat from * across row, ending with 2A. Add 17 stacks total, with 2 stacks in the last loop.

Row 9: Catch the second loop. With A, work 16 stacks.

Row 10: Catch the second loop. With A, work 15 stacks.

Add Swag Fringe

Row 1: Continuing with working thread, string 30 beads and go up through the outermost bead on the opposite end of this row. Pass needle down through the next bead in the row.

Row 2: String 24 beads and go up through the second bead from the end on the opposite end of the row. Pass needle down through the next bead in the row.

Row 3: String 18 beads and go up through the third bead from the opposite end of the row. Pass needle down through the next bead in the row. Weave your thread back and forth through several beads and clip the thread close to the beadwork.

Add Supports to Tops of Telsem

With thread coming out of the sixth bead from the left of the top row, add one rondelle, one

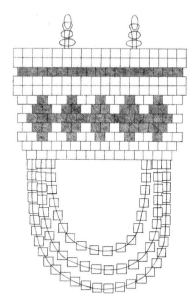

3 mm round bead and one rondelle (this rondelle will stand on its edge and be strung on the main supporting strand later). Go back through the round bead and the first rondelle and back into the bead you started from in the top row. Weave your thread through the beadwork until the thread is coming out of the sixth bead from the right of the top row and add supporting beads as for the left side.

Stringing Beads

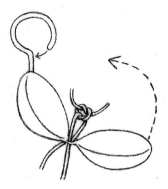

Pass the FF cord through the loop of the floss threader. Bring the two ends together, knot, and melt or apply nail polish to the knot. Pass the threader

You may also make telsem in a triangular shape.

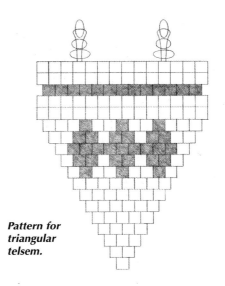

Pattern for
triangular
telsem.

through the bead tip so the knot sits inside the cup. String on eleven 6 mm round Bali silver beads alternating with eleven plain silver round beads. *Pass threader through first support of a telsem, add a tubular silver bead, then pass through the second support. Add a plain silver round bead, a Bali silver bead, and a round bead. Repeat from * until all seven

telsem have been strung. String beads for the second half of the necklace (mirror image of first half) beginning with a plain silver round bead and ending with a Bali silver bead. Pass the threader through the second bead tip from the outside of the cup to the inside. Cut the thread from the threader, knot ends together with a square knot, and melt or apply nail polish to the knot.

Close both bead tips around the knots. Connect the bead tip to the clasp.

Egyptian Amulet Purse

The inspiration for this amulet purse came from a bracelet worn by Egyptian Queen Aahotep (18th Dynasty, c 1540 BC). It was made of gold, turquoise, lapis lazuli, and carnelian beads. This bag is made with flat brick stitch, which is sewn up the side edge to form a tube.

Supplies

Red (R), gold (G) and blue (B) seed beads or
  cylinder beads, 5 grams each
Gold thread
72 blue 4 mm round beads
24 red 4 mm round beads
7 gold faceted beads for fringe
Egyptian charms such as lotus flower, Cleo-
  patra's snake, Eye of Horus or other.

Work flat brick stitch (see pages 32–36) in seed or cylinder beads following the chart on page 92 or the written instructions, catching the first loop of every row. **Note:** *The front and back of the bag (right and left sides as it is worked) are slightly different.* The symbols → and ← indicate in which direction the row is worked.

Row 1 → : 2B, 19G, 2B, 1G, 2B, 19G, 2B, 1G

Row 2 ← : 1G, 2B, 1G, 18R, (1G, 2B × 2), 19R, 2B

Row 3 → : 2B, (1G, 2R X 6), (1G, 2B × 2), (1G, 2R × 6), 1G, 2B, 1G

Row 4 ← : 1G, 2B, (2G, 1R × 6), 2G, (2B, 1G × 2), (1R, 2G × 5), 1R, 1G, 2B

Row 5 → : 2B, 19G, 2B, 1G, 2B, 19G, 2B, 1G

Row 6 ← : 1G, 2B, 1G, 18B, 1G, 2B, 1G, 22B

Row 7 → : (2B, 1G × 16)

Row 8 ← : 1G, 2B, (2G, 1B × 6), 2G, (2B, 1G × 2), (1B, 2G × 5), 1B, 1G, 2B

Repeat Rows 1–8 three more times.

Form the Bag

Weave the two side edges together to form a tube, then sew across the bottom edge as shown. Add fringe to the solid gold area of

the bottom edge. This bag has fringe in the first and last bead and every third bead between.

Strap

To make the neck strap, anchor two 2-yd threads to one top side edge of the bag. The thread will be used double and each thread will be on its own needle. *Thread both needles through a round blue bead. String 7 gold seed beads on each thread. Thread both needles through a round red bead. Repeat from * 11 more times.

On one thread, string 7 gold seed beads, pass through a round blue bead, string 7 gold seed beads. With the other thread, string 14 gold seed beads, pass through 1 round blue bead, string 1 charm, pass back through the round blue bead, string 14 gold seed beads.

Pass both threads through 1 round red bead. String a mirror image sequence of beads for the other side and secure both threads to the opposite side of the bag. Add a charm to embellish the bag.

Projects

91

Egyptian Amulet Purse

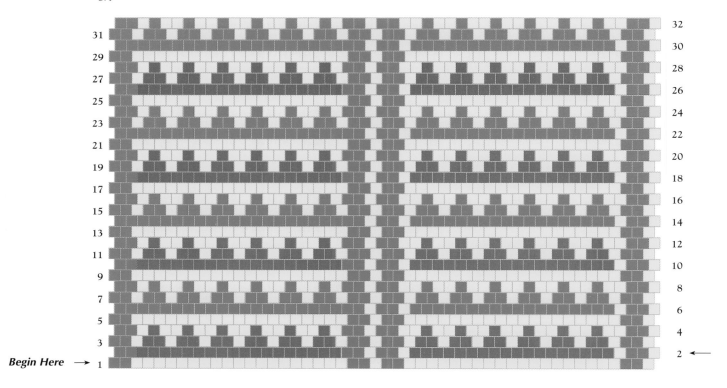

31
29
27
25
23
21
19
17
15
13
11
9
7
5
3

Begin Here → 1

32
30
28
26
24
22
20
18
16
14
12
10
8
6
4
2 ←

free-form Brick Stitch

If you like abstract art and letting yourself go, free-form brick stitch is for you. For many people, free-form work comes naturally while others prefer the control of mapping out their design in advance and knowing exactly what comes next. If you're in the latter category, there are some ways to make free-form a little less daunting.

Bonnie Voelker

The most important thing about a free-form piece is selecting a color palette. Color is the one element that will tie your piece together and keep it from looking like a mishmash. Your color palette should include light, medium, and dark colors and a bright or accent color. Choose a variety of sizes, shapes (triangle, hex, round), and finishes to give your piece texture and interest. Add a few large accent beads or other unusual elements such as a shell, a button, or other bauble and you're ready to begin.

One way to get started is to take a pencil and just doodle on paper for awhile. Or look for an abstract painting for inspiration. Then create those shapes with brick stitch using the techniques shown on pages 36–40 for increasing and decreasing.

Make a small piece of brick stitch with just a few rows, then begin to increase by

Joanne Hite

Alois Powers

making two stitches where there was one or by using larger beads. You'll notice that your piece begins to curve, ruffle or flair out. Keep going with an extension row using different

Alois Powers

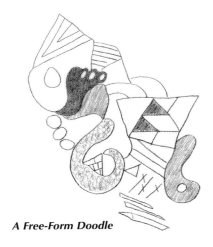

A Free-Form Doodle

beads. Add a large bead, shell, or other element and make a row around it using the base row technique.

When you've worked out a little area, begin again with other beads from your assortment. Don't hesitate to make layers or to decrease suddenly to shape your piece. If you hit a blank wall and don't know what to do next with your piece, pick a word or two from the list below to trigger an idea.

fringes	sparkle	depth
ruffles	holes	contrast
arcs	ovals	matte
squares	flashes	transparency
lines	puffs	encrusting
triangles	waves	repetition
points	meandering	iridescence
fanciful	mysterious	motion
rhythm	wavy lines	tension
tactile	sensuous	mystic
lacy	nature	amoeba
primary	lightning	geometric
emergence	metallic	blazing
illusion	black holes	bridges

Gallery

Diane Fitzgerald
Minneapolis, Minnesota.
Dragonflies. 7"W × 10"L.

Increasing brick stitch with Delica and
round seed beads, netted diamond
with glass stones, cluster of 3 mm
round glass beads, and dragonfly pins.

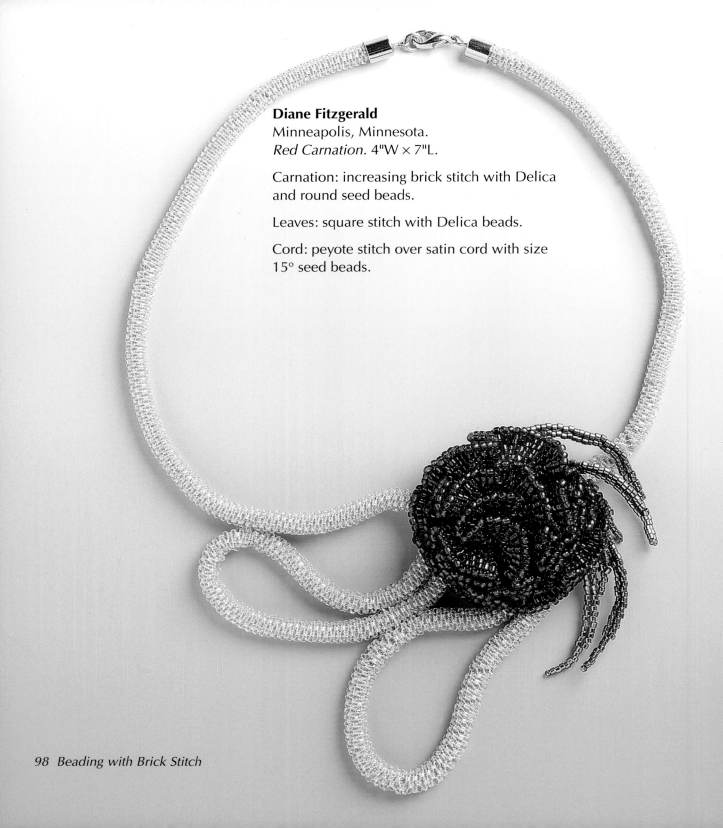

Diane Fitzgerald
Minneapolis, Minnesota.
Red Carnation. 4"W × 7"L.

Carnation: increasing brick stitch with Delica and round seed beads.

Leaves: square stitch with Delica beads.

Cord: peyote stitch over satin cord with size 15° seed beads.

Diane Fitzgerald
Minneapolis,
Minnesota.
Lily Pond.
6"W × 9½"L.

Increasing brick
stitch with Delica
beads, charms, and
found objects.

Support: figure 8
chain with Delica
and size 15° seed
beads.

Gallery 99

Diane Fitzgerald
Minneapolis, Minnesota.
*Morning Glory
Necklace.* 6"W × 8"L.

Flower: increasing brick
stitch with Delica beads.

Support: three-bead
netting with 3 mm
imitation pearls.

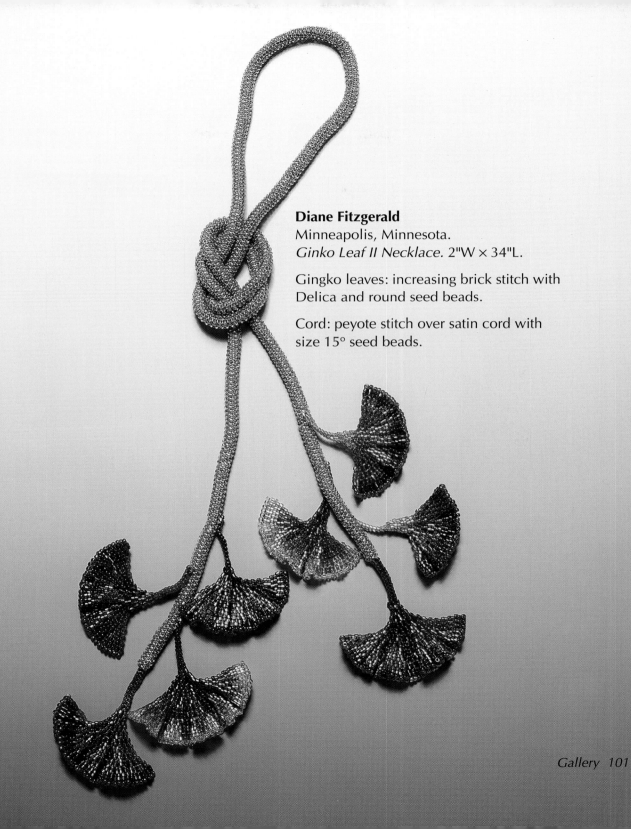

Diane Fitzgerald
Minneapolis, Minnesota.
Ginko Leaf II Necklace. 2"W × 34"L.

Gingko leaves: increasing brick stitch with
Delica and round seed beads.

Cord: peyote stitch over satin cord with
size 15° seed beads.

Diane Fitzgerald
Minneapolis, Minnesota.
Black Triangle Necklace.
1"W × 26"L.

Brick stitch triangles with size
8° hex beads.

Diane Fitzgerald
Minneapolis, Minnesota.
Cockade Hat Pin.
2½"W × 3"L.

Hat: increasing brick stitch with Delica beads.

Face: precious metal clay.

Tendrils: fringe with Delica and size 15° seed beads.

Diane Fitzgerald
Minneapolis,
Minnesota.
Caucasian Carpet.
5"W × 8"L.

Brick stitch with Delica beads.

Fringe: size 8° and size 15° seed beads.

JoAnn Baumann
Glencoe, Illinois.
Menopausal Mama.
12"W × 12"D × 22"H.

Brick stitch with thread
bobbins and silk fabric
strips.

Carol Perrenoud
Wilsonville, Oregon.
Road Warrior Bracelets. ¾"W × 6¾"L.

Brick stitch with Delica 3.3 beads and Czech
pressed glass bead pendants and drops.
Inspired by Sally Squire.

Fran Stone
Portland, Oregon.
Necklace.
6¾"W × 7"H.

Pin. (upper left)
3"W × 1½"H.

Pin. (upper right)
2¾"W × 1¾"H.

Brick stitch with
approximately size
11° twist beads.

Rachel Weiss
Charleston,
South Carolina.
*Mayan-Inca Necklace
and Earrings.*
8¼" W ¥ 5¾ H" plus strap.

Brick stitch with Delica
beads. Pieces connected
with garnets and gold-
filled beads. Based on
Mayan-Inca weavings.
Photograph by Rick Rhodes

NanC Meinhardt
Highland Park, Illinois.
Transparent Vessel. 6"W × 6"D × 5"H.

Mainly brick stitch with various seed beads.
Photograph by Tom Van Eynde

Denise Perreault
Boulder, Colorado.
Medieval Village. 48"L × 25"D.

Curtain of two-drop brick stitch
with seed beads.

Gini Williams Scalise
Winston-Salem, North Carolina.
Zelda Mae Was Queen of the Harvest Ball.
6½"W × 48"L plus fringe.

Combination of loomwork, peyote, African helix, ladder, and brick stitch with seed and bugle beads. Fruits (except grapes) are brick stitch.

Joanne Hite
Coon Rapids, Minnesota.
Untitled.
7"W × 6¼"H plus strap.

Brick stitch with seed beads
and cabochon.

Joanne Hite
Coon Rapids, Minnesota.
Petroglyph Gourd.
6¼"H × 6¼"W.

Joanne adapted Diane
Fitzgerald's Petroglyph
Necklace (see page 58) to
decorate a gourd.

Paulette Baron
Potomac, Maryland.
Wild Women.
1¼" to 1½"W by 3⅛" to 4¾"H.

Free-form sculptural brick stitch with
various beads.

Margo C. Field
Albuquerque, New Mexico.
La Borborleta Clara.
10"W × 12½"H.

Brick stitch wings on peyote body
with seed beads.

Peggy Wright
St. Paul, Minnesota.
Bargello Bliss Necklace.
7¾"W × 3"H plus straps.

Brick stitch with Delica beads.

Ann Gilbert
Minneapolis, Minnesota.
Goddess of the Garden.
4"W × 12"H plus base.

One-, two-, and three-drop brick
stitch with size 11° seed beads.

Cheryl Erickson
West Des Moines, Iowa.
Untitled. 9½"W × 10½"H.

Free-form brick stitch necklace with blue and metallic beads.

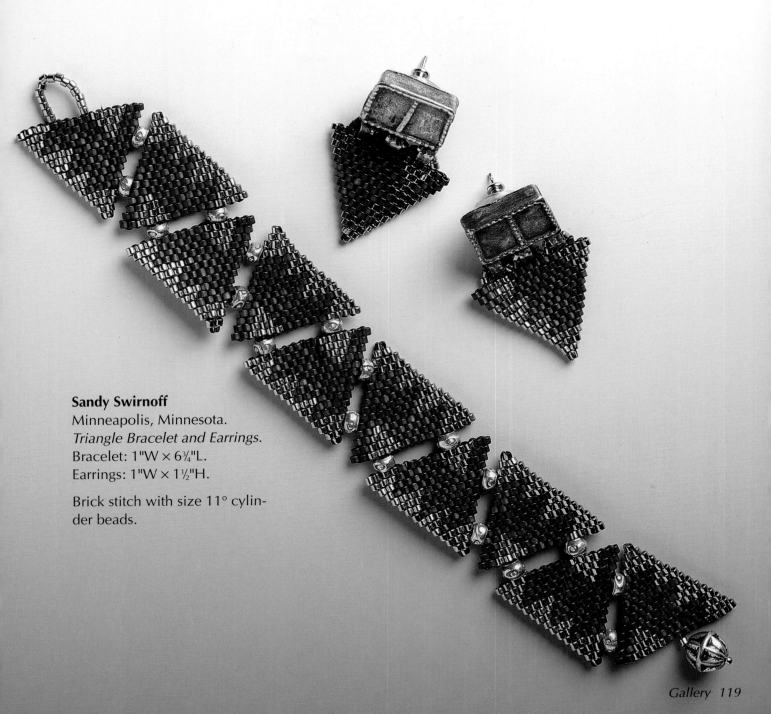

Sandy Swirnoff
Minneapolis, Minnesota.
Triangle Bracelet and Earrings.
Bracelet: 1"W × 6¾"L.
Earrings: 1"W × 1½"H.

Brick stitch with size 11° cylinder beads.

Mary Lou Allen
Sturgeon Bay, Wisconsin.
Butterfly Vase. 3½"W × 6¼"H.

Brick stitch butterfly on vase covered
with various techniques.

Carole Horn
New York, New York.
Butterfly Pins.
2½"W × 3"H.

Brick, peyote, and herringbone stitches with various seed beads.

Doris Coghill
Jordan, Minnesota.
Beaded Pot.
3½"W × 2¾"H.

Brick stitch with various beads
over glass pot.

Jill Cremer
Mission Viejo, California.
Monarchs: Banner of America.
24"W × 36"H.

Brick stitched butterflies mounted
on eucalyptus branches.

Beaded by Randee Barr, Sharon
Bernheimer, Leila Collar, Bonnie
Copeland, Jill Cremer, Bellie Frankel,
Suzanne Harmon, D'elin Lohr,
Sharon Mazzoni, A.K. Plummer, Tracy
Sherwood, Paulette Smith, and
Annetta Vernon.
Photograph by Lexie Harvey

Alois Powers
St. Paul, Minnesota.
Wavy Line Bracelets.
¾" to 1⅛"W × 7½" to 8¼"L.

Brick stitch with cylinder, round, and
triangle beads.

Joanne Hite
Coon Rapids,
Minnesota.
Joanne's Little Men.
1¼"W × 4¼"H.

Purple clown by
Peggy Wright, orange
and black patterned
man by Jane Langen-
back, and Santa by
Diane Fitzgerald.

Bibliography and Resources

Aikman, Z. Susanne. *A Primer: The Art of Native American Beadwork.* Denver: Morning Flower Press, 1980.

Alford, Susan. "Double Donut Pendant." *Bead & Button,* October 1999, pp. 32–35.

Arnoldi, Mary Jo and Christine Mullen Kreamer. *Crowning Achievements: African Arts of Dressing the Head.* Los Angeles: Fowler Museum of Cultural History, 1995.

Barnett, Beverly. *Bugle Beading.* Ft. Worth, Texas. Design Originals (#1035) 1992.

Bast, Joanne Strehle. "Button and Bead Brooches." *Bead and Button,* February 2000, pp. 38–40.

Bateman, Sharon. "Half-round Earrings." *Bead & Button,* October 1999, pp. 36–37.

Berry, Lori S. *How to Bead Earrings: An Artistic Approach.* Liberty, Utah: Eagle's View Publishing, 1993.

Blakelock, Virginia. *Those Bad, Bad Beads.* Wilsonville, Oregon: Universal Synergetics, 1988.

Collier, Carole. *The Three-Bead Brick Stitch Necklace Expressions.* New York: Carole Collier, 1998.

DeLange, Deon. *Beaded Treasure Purses: Tubular Brick Stitch Designs.* Liberty, Utah: Eagle's View Publishing, 1997.

———. *More Techniques of Beading Earrings.* Liberty, Utah: Eagle's View Publishing, 1985.

———. *Techniques of Beading Earrings.* Liberty, Utah: Eagle's View Publishing, 1984.

———. *Techniques of Fashion Earrings.* Liberty, Utah: Eagle's View Publishing, 1995.

Elbe, Barbara E. *Amulet Obsessions.* Redding, California: B.E.E. Publishing, 1998.

———. *Beaded Images: Intricate Beaded Jewelry Using Brick Stitch.* Liberty, Utah: Eagle's View Publishing, 1995.

———. *Beaded Images II: Intricate Beaded Jewelry Using Brick Stitch.* Liberty, Utah: Eagle's View Publishing, 1996.

———. *Back to Beadin'.* Redding, California: B.E.E. Publishing, 1996.

Fitzgerald, Diane. *Counted and Charted Patterns for Flat Peyote Stitch.* Beautiful Beads Press, 1995 (These patterns may be used for brick stitch as well.)

Goodhue, Horace. *Indian Bead-Weaving Patterns.* St. Paul, Minnesota: Bead-Craft, 1989.

Hixon, Valerie. *Bloomin' Beads.* Grass Valley, California: Hixson Studios. 1999.

Hughes, Charlene. *Beadin' with Beady Boop.* Eureka, California: Beady Boop, 1999.

Jones, Mrs. C. S. and Henry T. Williams. *Ladies Fancywork: Hints and Helps to Home Taste and Recreations.* New York: Henry T. Williams, 1876.

Louise, Irene. *Cheyenne Stitch Earrings: Garden Edition, Flowers, Butterflies and Birdhouses,* Vol. 4. Greenbank, Washington: Irene Louise Designs, P.O. Box 51, 98253.

May, Nola. *Classic Earring Designs.* Liberty, Utah: Eagle's View Publishing, 1994.

Neuwirth, Waltraud, *Perlen Aus Gablonz.* Bad Vöslau, Austria: Waltraud Neuwirth, 1994.

Radford, Jan. *Delightful Beaded Earring Designs.* Liberty, Utah: Eagle's View Publishing, 1994.

Reid, Laura. *Adventures in Creating Earrings.* Liberty, Utah: Eagle's View Publishing, 1994.

———. *New Adventures in Beading Earrings.* Liberty, Utah: Eagle's View Publishing, 1990.

Revault, Jacques. *Designs and Patterns from North American Carpets and Textiles.* New York: Dover Publications, Inc., 1973.

Sova, Rita. *Butterfly and Fairy Designs.* Albuquerque, New Mexico: Rita Sova, 1998.

———. *Angel Designs.* Albuquerque, New Mexico: Rita Sova, 1998.

Steil, Starr. *Picture Beaded Earrings for Beginners.* Liberty, Utah: Eagle's View Publishing, 1995.

Wells, Carol Wilcox. *Creative Bead Weaving.* Asheville, North Carolina: Lark Books, 1996.

Wynne-Evans, Sigrid. *Earring Designs by Sig* I. Liberty, Utah: Eagle's View Publishing, 1992.

———. *Earring Designs by Sig* II. Liberty, Utah: Eagle's View Publishing, 1993.

Paisley Resources

Carlson, Linda. "Paisley Shawls." *Piecework,* Vol. VI, No. 6; Nov./Dec. 1998, pp. 46–51.

Clabburn, Pamela. *Shawls.* United Kingdom: Shire Publications, Ltd., 1981.

Levi-Strauss, Monique. *The Cashmere Shawl.* New York: Harry N. Abrams, 1988.

Mirow, Gregory. *Paisley Giftwrap Paper.* New York: Dover Publications, Inc., 1989.

———. *Paisley Designs: 44 Original Plates.* New York: Dover Publications, Inc., 1989.

The Paisley Pattern, The Official Illustrated History. Salt Lake City: Peregrine Smith Books, 1987.

Parker, Freda. *Victorian Embroidery.* New York: Crescent Books, 1990. pp. 64–68.

Ratti and Paisley. New York: Fashion Institute of Technology, 1987.

Reilly, Valerie. *Paisley Patterns.* New York: Crown Publishers, 1989.

Rossbach, Ed. *The Art of Paisley.* New York: Van Nostrand Reinhold, 1980.

Walsh, Margaret and Augustine Hope. *Living Colors: The Definitive Guide to Color Palettes Through the Ages.* San Francisco: Chronicle Books, 1995.

Other References

Andrews, Carol. *Ancient Egyptian Jewelry.* New York: Harry N. Abrams, Inc. 1990

Barth, Georg J. *Native American Beadwork.* Stevens Point, Wisconsin: R. Schneider, Publishers, 1993.

Carey, Margret. *Beads and Beadwork of East and South Africa.* Buckinghamshire, United Kingdom: Shire Publications, Ltd., 1986.

———. *Beads and Beadwork of West and Central Africa.* Buckinghamshire, United Kingdom: Shire Publications, Ltd., 1991.

Dubin, Lois Sherr. *North American Indian Jewelry and Adornment.* New York: Harry N. Abrams, Inc. 1999.

Holm, Edith. *Glasperlen.* Munich: Verlag George D. W. Callwey, 1984.

Lubar, Steven, and W. David Kingery, eds. *History From Things: Essays on Material Culture.* Washington, D.C.: Smithsonian Institution Press, 1993.

Orchard, William C. *Beads and Beadwork of the American Indians.* New York: Museum of the American Indian Heye Foundation, 1975.

Parker, Freda. *Victorian Embroidery.* New York: Crescent Books, 1991.

Schoeman, Stan. A *Brief History of Traditional African Bead Craft.* http://minotaur.marques.co.za/ clients/zulu/history.htm: 1996.

Skotnes, Pippa. *Miscast: Negotiating the Presence of the Bushmen.* Capetown, South Africa: University of Capetown Press, 1996.

Whiteford, Andrew Hunter. *North American Indian Arts.* New York: Golden Press, 1970, 1990.

Wilson, Eva. *Ancient Egyptian Designs for Artists and Craftspeople.* New York: Dover Publications, Inc., 1986.

Other Books by Diane Fitzgerald

These books are available from Beautiful Beads Press, 115 Hennepin Ave., Minneapolis, MN 55401.

Beads & Threads: A New Technique for Fiber Jewelry, with co-author Helen Banes

Counted and Charted Patterns for Flat Peyote Stitch

More Zulu Beadwork

Sea Anemone Beadwork

Zulu Beaded Chain Techniques

Index

BEADWORK Magazine

BEADWORK magazine is devoted to every kind of bead stitching and creating. Its pages are filled with the latest innovations of the craft, including seed bead stitching, wirework, lampwork, and bead knitting, crochet, and embroidery. BEADWORK features beautiful photographs and drawings that illustrate projects designed by beadworkers all over the world. Its artist profiles, tips, calendar, and reviews allow readers to keep their fingers on the pulse of the international bead community. $24.95 (6 issues) 800-340-7496.

BEADWORK How-To Books

Our popular line of BEADWORK How-To books are inspirational as well as technical. Get started on learning a specific stitch or technique with incredibly detailed instructions and superb line drawings. Providing fuel for the fire are the gallery of works created by the authors and contemporary artists in full-color photography.

8½ × 9, paperbound, 128 pages.
ISBN: 1-883010-63-2— $21.95

8½ × 9, paperbound, 112 pages.
ISBN: 1-883010-73-X — $21.95

8½ × 9, paperbound, 112 pages.
ISBN: 1-883010-71-3 — $21.95

**Look
for INTERWEAVE
books at your favorite
book or bead store,
or call (800) 272-2193,
Visit us online at
www.interweave.com**